The Lady
& Sons,
Too!

PAULA DEEN

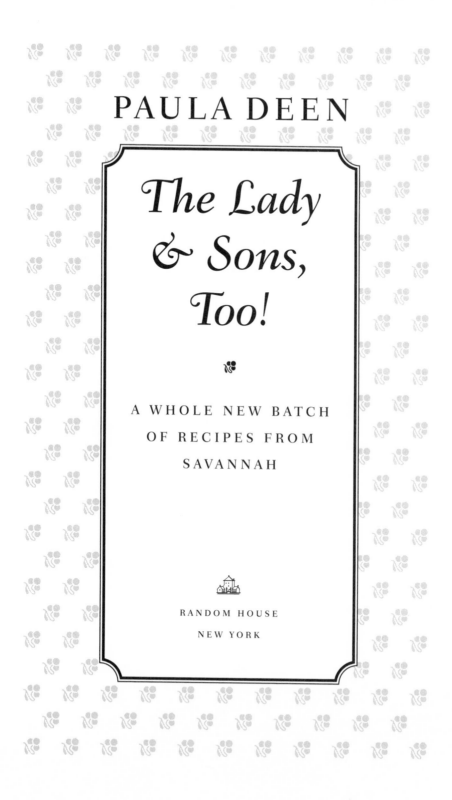

The Lady & Sons, Too!

A WHOLE NEW BATCH
OF RECIPES FROM
SAVANNAH

RANDOM HOUSE

NEW YORK

*I'm so fortunate to be blessed with three wonderful
men in my life, men who have given to me their
unconditional love and support.
These men are my sons, Jamie and Bobby Deen,
and my brother, Earl W. Hiers, Jr. (Bubba),
to whom this book is most affectionately dedicated.*

Acknowledgments

To all my family, friends, staff, and guests who have given their invaluable help in making this book and restaurant a reality. My most heartfelt thanks go out to each and every one of you: John and Carol Berendt, Jack H. Biel, Travis Blackshear, John Brown, Dian Brownfield, Sharon Bruggeman, Lori Burnett, Lisa Calcaine, Bobbi I. Cappelli, Dora Charles, Tracy Clark, Sandra Cowan, Roger Crews, Stephanie Crystal, Carolyn Cundiff, Peggy Deen, Phil Donaldson, Lawrence Duncan, Susan Dupuy, Ann G. Fisch, Rodney Floyd, Damon Lee Fowler, Levita and Ron Garner, Rick Gnann, Steve Green, Lori Greenlee, Tracey Gribbon, Anne Hanson, Bubba Hiers, James Hodges, Patricia Hoisington, Brenda B. Hollis, Angie Hopper, Jeanne Hungerpillar, Bunny Hutchins, Rance Jackson, Ineata Jones, Virgil Kummero, Anne Landers, Audanta Lewis, John Lucas, Jude Mathews, Louis (Trey) Mathews III, Barbara McChesney, Laura Miller, Marilyn Milson, Renee Mincey, Donna Mobley, Delonzo Moody, Jackie Mullins, Catherine Nadeau, Stacey Nelson, Martha Gidden Nesbit, Zeide Nuss, Kelly Ort, Peggy Ort, Patrick Otis, Ingrid Parker, Donna Pichard, Ginger Pitts, Robert Pleasanton, Mary H. Plyler, Byron Polite, Charles Polite, Helen Rooks, Barbara Russell, Bruce and Carolyn Ryder, Vickie Sepielli, Esther Shaver, Michelle and Bruce Shelar, Kristen Short, Martha (Betty) Smith, Donna Sparks, Amanda Stephens, Cathy Stephens, Jeffery Stevens, Polly Powers Stramm, Bobbie Strong, Elizabeth Terry, Herb Traub, Donald Wade, Suzette Wagner, Dustin Walls, Tom Walsh, Doris Warren, Serna Wilkes, and Lucile Wright.

I would especially like to express thanks for the wonderful care and consideration Random House has given me in transforming what started off as a collection of local recipes into a national cookbook—it has been a dream come true. Since discovering The Lady & Sons on a business trip, my editor, Pamela Cannon, has worked tirelessly on the books' behalf, for which I thank her a thousand times over. I would also like to express my gratitude to: Beth Pearson, Janet Wygal, Vicki Wong, Stacy Rockwood, Kathy Rosenbloom, Krista Vossen, and Christina Figel.

Contents

The Journey Continues . . .

When I look back over my life, I get filled with so much emotion. My early childhood and teen years were so wonderful and safe. My brother, Bubba, and I were protected, guided, and watched over by wonderful parents. You get so secure that you begin to think life is made up of only peaks and almost no valleys. I was nineteen, and Bubba was twelve, when our father, who was our hero, died unexpectedly at the age of forty. This was the beginning of my broken spirit. When our beautiful, sweet, and loving mother died four years later at the age of forty-four, I felt impending doom hanging over me. I thought this valley would last for years.

Being married with two babies under the age of three and a sixteen-year-old brother to finish raising was a big task for a twenty-three-year-old girl. I certainly couldn't classify myself as a woman because I think my mental growth froze at the age of nineteen from the pure shock of the situation. While trying very hard to put up a competent front, I became a scared, nervous shell of my usual self. I lived in dreadful fear of the death of someone I loved, or my own death.

In 1978, due to tremendous financial problems, my husband and I lost our business and also our home. It was at this point, after getting situated into an apartment, that I began to feel safe only within the four walls of my own home. Before long, I had stopped doing anything that required me to leave the apartment. The very thought of having to leave my safety zone sent me into a horrendous panic attack. During these attacks my arms would go numb and my heart would almost pound out of my chest, leaving me weak.

Surely this had to be the death that I had been waiting for. The fear of the fear eventually made me a virtual prisoner. Life continued much the same way for the next nine or ten years. Then, like a miracle, at the age of forty, I got up one day and felt as if a light had been turned on. Yes, one day I would die and I might possibly lose others that I loved, but that was all out of my control. God had given me today, and today I would start the journey of mending. We all know that a certain amount of fear is natural, that healthy fear keeps us safe, but I never again would let myself be a victim of controlling fear.

Sometimes I feel as though I have two birthdays: one January 19, 1947, and the other June 19, 1989. The second date marks the day that I became completely responsible for myself and my actions; it was the day that I, with the help of my sons, Jamie and Bobby, began our business. All those years of being a prisoner in my home were about to pay off, for I had become a pretty good cook. After all, cooking had been my number-one source of entertainment.

The business was started with just two hundred dollars, and today I can still tell you, almost to the penny, how I spent it all. The first year and a half was spent working out of our home, and this proved to be quite a hardship for the family. A divorce after twenty-seven years of marriage was imminent, and we were about to tackle a full-fledged restaurant as well. The next five years would be the hardest, physically, that I had ever experienced. I had taken an available space located in the Best Western Central Motel, and the restaurant required three meals a day, seven days a week.

There was no money to pay employees, so I, along with Jamie, Bobby, and their girlfriends, began the task of providing good, afford-able food for our guests. Soon (although it seemed like forever) I was able to employ some very talented women. They were wonderful cooks, and all I needed to do was show them how I wanted things prepared. Almost immediately they were off and running and before long they were teaching me things as well!

Jamie and Bobby were waiters and enjoyed a nice boost to their income through their tips, but the size of the restaurant would not allow me to generate the income I had hoped for. I dreamed of something bigger, a place where my style of food went hand-in-hand with its surroundings. We had met and made friends with many wonderful people on the south side of Savannah, but I knew that we belonged downtown.

It was time to take the next step. I had not a clue just how hard that next step would prove to be. Being naïve, I signed a long-term lease on a wonderful old building in the heart of historic Savannah. It would require total renovation—all at my expense! It's amazing, but when I signed that lease it never dawned on me that I might not be able to get the financing; after all, I had saved and scraped up $20,000, and surely that was good for something. Our nonrenewable lease with the Best Western expired and all we had now was the catering part of the business to keep things going. Bank after bank refused my applications, despite my tears and pleas, until the day I met Doug McCoy, vice president of one of the local banks. Doug listened to my plan and gave me great encouragement. He suggested that with a loan from his bank and the help of SBA and SBAC, we could probably put together a package. The encouragement was short-lived though, because although I had $20,000 in savings, I was still short $25,000. One thing was definite: This was another valley. I had no idea where to turn, but then my mentors and most enthusiastic cheerleaders stepped up and helped clear the way for me and my sons. My aunt Peggy and uncle George Ort did something for which we will be forever grateful. They lent us the remaining money, making it possible for us to open a wonderful restaurant and meet the world—and what a world it was! Our trials were certainly not over, but there was light at the end of the tunnel. On the morning of opening day I received a call from our accountant, Karl Schumacher, who said, "Paula, we're in pretty bad trouble here. Both the construction and restaurant accounts are overdrawn, and we need to take care of this." Well, I hadn't had any money to put in the parking meters that day, much less to cover the overdrafts. In fact, I didn't have a penny to make change with. We were supposed to open our brand-new business in less than an hour—how could I cash a check on an overdrawn account? I made a humbling phone call to my banker and explained the situation and asked him to please allow me to cash just one more check. With a smile in his voice he said, "Yes, Paula, come on down and get your start-up change. We're not going this far with you to stop you now. Good luck!" I'm extremely proud to say that that was the last time we were overdrawn.

That opening lunch was very emotional indeed. It had been almost a year since we had served a guest in-house. The wonderful and loyal friends we had made on the south side magically appeared in an outpouring of support. You all know who you are, and I'll never be able to convey to you my thanks. We enjoyed seeing our old friends, and we soon began adding new friends, some here for only a short visit, some who make their daily living in the downtown area. The number of familiar faces continues to grow.

The next step in my plan was to write and publish a cookbook. Once more I saved $20,000, and soon the cookbook became a reality, not just a dream. My self-published book had been out for only two weeks when another new face appeared. It belonged to a wonderful young woman named Pamela Cannon, an editor at Random House. I can't tell you the surprise and shock I felt the day Pamela called me from New York and said that Random House wanted to publish and distribute my cookbook nationwide. Was I interested? As you probably know by now, the answer was yes.

This was definitely a peak. Pamela has worked tirelessly on my books, and not only do I consider her a talented editor, but a friend who I'm very glad to know. Thank you, Pamela, for being you.

One of the more recent arrivals in our life is a man named Jerry Shriver, who has had a tremendous impact on our business. Jerry is a food and travel writer for *USA Today*. Our meeting was not planned. He was visiting Savannah for the weekend to judge a food extravaganza. When he checked into the Mulberry Inn, Louise Purdy, the concierge, suggested that he might want to drop into The Lady & Sons Restaurant for a sample of "real good" Southern cooking. He did just that. Imagine our amazement on December 17, 1999, when Mr. Shriver's *USA Today* article appeared, declaring that his number-one most memorable meal of the year 1999 had been at The Lady & Sons.

How does one go about expressing one's gratitude for something like that? Along with a heartfelt "thank you" to Jerry, I would also like to say I'm elated that he has been a part of my journey.

In fact, there are many people I would like to thank. Our employees, who give a special piece of themselves every day—you help make it all happen. The guests who come in from far away—you're unbelievable. You all bring such pleasure to us. It's truly been an honor to serve each and every one of y'all. To our local friends—your faces are dear to us, your loyalty and support are so very much appreciated by Jamie, Bobby, me, and the staff. We look forward to serving you all for many years to come.

A very special thanks goes to my dear friend and assistant, Sandra

Cowan. She probably has the hardest job of all, trying to cover my tracks. My lack of organization and order is enough to send anyone over the edge, but Sandra manages it beautifully and always with a smile. Thank you, Sandra, for always being willing to go the extra mile.

I often wonder how one woman could be so blessed. Not only am I no longer a prisoner in my home, but I have been hopping on a plane every six weeks for more than a year now to appear on QVC to promote *The Lady & Sons Savannah Country Cookbook,* and this effort has been hugely successful.

I'm in a business that allows me to stay close to my children and brings wonderful new friends into our lives on a daily basis. Now, at this age and stage of my life, I understand that life does consist of peaks and valleys. The valleys help to mold us into the people we are; without them we would not be able to relish and enjoy the peaks, or be able to know the difference. It is not the destination but the journey.

And so the journey continues . . .

Paula Deen

P.S. By the way, my dear brother, Bubba, has made it beautifully through his own peaks and valleys. Our parents would be so proud of him and his precious children.

If you are lucky enough to be in the Savannah area, we would love for you to stop by the restaurant. Please visit us at:

The Lady & Sons
102 West Congress Street
Savannah, GA 31401
(912) 233-2600
www.ladyandsons.com

If you can't get to Savannah to sample the wonderful food at The Lady & Sons, you can still taste the dishes at home. The recipes in this book that we have served at our restaurant or plan on adding to our menu are followed by:

🐾 🐾 🐾 *The Lady & Sons*

You can now take the wonderful tastes of The Lady & Sons home with you! We have developed a line of food products that are available from our website (www.ladyandsons.com) or from QVC. Our products include: The Lady's Seasoned Salt, The Lady's House Seasoning, The Lady's Insane Salt, and The Lady's Bake Mix. Many of the recipes in this book use these products, and I certainly recommend them for the most flavor and best results. But if you're in a pinch, you can make do with the following substitutes: For The Lady's House Seasoning, substitute the House Seasoning recipe (see page 141). For The Lady's Seasoned Salt, substitute Lawry's Seasoned Salt. For The Lady's Insane Salt, substitute Jane's Krazy Mixed-Up Salt.

Helpful Hints
from The Lady

1. When using muffin tins, if you find you don't have enough batter to fill all the cups, pour a little water into empty ones. This will prevent the pan from scorching.

2. To sanitize cutting boards and countertops, use a mixture of 1 tablespoon bleach to 1 gallon of water.

3. Don't throw away stale bread; cut it up and use it for croutons or breadcrumbs.

4. Find yourself with more eggs than you can use before the date expires? Break the eggs into ice cube trays, separating the white into one cube and the yolk into another cube, mixing with a pinch of salt or sugar per yolk. 3 tablespoons of beaten egg equal 1 whole egg; 2 tablespoons of egg white plus 1 tablespoon of yolk equal 1 large egg. Cover and freeze for future use, up to 1 month.

5. To slice a cheesecake without a lot of mess, use a piece of dental floss a few inches longer than the diameter of the cake. Wrap the floss around your fingers tightly and press down and through the cake. Release one end of the floss and pull through the cake. Repeat until the entire cake is sliced.

6. When baking a pie, if you find your crust is browning too fast, wrap strips of tin foil around the edge of the pie to slow down the browning.

7. When making muffins, avoid overmixing. Use a spoon to mix the batter; never use an electric mixer.

8. If you have overbaked your cake layers, make a simple syrup of 1 cup sugar, 1 cup water, and 1 teaspoon vanilla; boil for 3 to 5 minutes, then brush the cake layers with syrup on both sides until they are "revived."

9. When picking crabmeat free of bits of shell, spread the crabmeat in a thin layer on a baking sheet and place it in a 350-degree oven for about 10 minutes. This will make it easier to see the bits of shell.

10. To deodorize jars, pour in a solution of 1 tablespoon of dry mustard and 1 gallon of warm water. To deodorize plastic containers, wad up newspaper, place it in the containers, cover, and let sit overnight.

11. When making meringue, always have the egg whites at room temperature, and be sure they're free of any trace of yolk. Make sure the bowl and beaters are spotless and totally free of grease.

12. If soup is too salty, add a teaspoon each of cider vinegar and sugar, or a whole peeled raw potato. Leave the potato in the soup and serve from around it.

13. To render more juice from a lemon, warm it in the microwave for 30 seconds on high power.

14. When boiling crab, shrimp, or any shellfish, add 1 tablespoon of vinegar to the water. This helps to loosen the meat from the shell.

15. Don't have any eggs for a baking recipe? Use 2 tablespoons of corn oil plus 1 tablespoon of water as a substitute.

16. Store eggs tapered-side down for longer life.

17. Soak chicken in 1 tablespoon of baking powder with enough water to cover the chicken. Soak for 10 to 15 minutes to discourage bacteria. Rinse chicken and cook thoroughly.

18. Use lemon or lime juice as a marinade to tenderize chicken.

19. Keep a plastic container in the freezer to store small amounts of leftover vegetables. When the container is full, pull it out and make a wonderful pot of vegetable soup.

20. When sautéing, always heat your pan before putting in the fat. This will temper the pan and reduce sticking.

21. For a crisp salad, take special care of your greens. For iceberg lettuce: Hit the bottom of the head of lettuce against your kitchen counter a

few times and then remove the core. Soak the head of lettuce in ice-cold water for 10 to 15 minutes and then drain. For romaine, red, or green leaf lettuce: Trim a thin layer off the bottom of the core; this will allow the lettuce to "drink" when it's soaking. Remove any outer wilted leaves. Soak each head in ice-cold water for 10 to 15 minutes. Store heads of lettuce in plastic bags with a few paper towels to absorb some of the moisture. Remember, when ready to make a salad, never cut your greens with a knife; instead, tear them gently.

22. When deep-fat frying, try adding a tablespoon of vinegar to the fat before heating. This will keep the food from absorbing too much of the fat.

23. Add 1 tablespoon of vinegar to beef stews to tenderize the meat.

24. When cooking green vegetables, add 1 teaspoon of lemon juice to the pot to help retain their color.

25. Don't salt fresh corn during cooking; salt will toughen it. Salt the corn to taste after it's cooked.

26. Add a little oil to the water when cooking pasta to keep the water from boiling over and the pasta from sticking together.

27. For extra-fluffy meringues, add ¼ teaspoon vinegar to 3 egg whites.

28. To make peaches easier to peel, drop them into a pot of boiling water and take them out after 1 minute. This also works for tomatoes: Leave them in for 1 to 2 minutes, or until their skins split.

29. When a recipe calls for chopped celery also include the celery leaves, which lend wonderful flavor and color.

30. To clean a toilet: Pour a can of Coca-Cola into the toilet bowl. Let the "real thing" sit for one hour, then flush clean. The citric acid in Coke removes stains from vitreous china.

31. To remove grease from clothes: Empty a can of Coca-Cola into a load of greasy clothes, add detergent, and run through a regular cycle. The Coca-Cola will help loosen grease stains.

32. And finally, treat your family like company and your company like family.

Appetizers

HOT APPETIZERS

Baked Cheese Spread

Hot Crab Dip

Polynesian Chicken Wings

Spinach and Shrimp Dip

Italian Chicken Sticks

Shore Is Good Seafood Dip

Sugar-and-Nut-Glazed Brie

Tomato Canapés

Mushroom Canapés

Artichoke Frittata

Chicken Nuggets

Black Bean Dip

COLD APPETIZERS

Shrimp Mold

South Georgia "Caviar"

Devilish Cheese Logs

Georgia Spiced Pecans

Tangy Marinated Shrimp

Caviar Spread

Candied Dills

"Boursin Cheese"

Herbed Cheese-and-Cracker Bits

Party Eye-of-Round Steak

Mexican Layered Dip

Salsa Chicken Salad

Smoked Oyster Cheese Balls

Zesty Cheese Straws

Stuffed French Bread

Egg Caviar Mold

Baked Cheese Spread

1 cup mayonnaise
1 cup grated Colby cheese
1 cup chopped onion

Dash of Tabasco sauce (optional)
Dash of Worcestershire sauce
(optional)

Preheat the oven to 350 degrees. Mix all ingredients in a pie plate. Bake until golden brown on top, about 30 minutes. Serve with crackers or bagel chips.

Hot Crab Dip

1 pound jumbo lump crabmeat,
   picked free of any broken shells
1 cup grated pepper Jack cheese
¾ cup mayonnaise
¼ cup freshly grated Parmesan
¼ cup minced green onions
   (optional)
5–6 cloves roasted garlic, or 2
cloves garlic, minced

3 tablespoons Worcestershire sauce
2 tablespoons fresh lemon or lime
   juice
1 teaspoon Tabasco sauce
½ teaspoon dry mustard
Salt and pepper

Preheat the oven to 325 degrees. Combine all of the ingredients in a casserole and gently stir until thoroughly mixed. Bake for 40 minutes. Serve hot with crackers or toast points.

Polynesian Chicken Wings

SERVES 12–15

3 pounds chicken wings
1 cup pineapple preserves
½ cup sherry
½ cup frozen orange juice
   concentrate

½ cup soy sauce
½ cup packed brown sugar
¼ cup vegetable oil
1 teaspoon garlic powder
1 teaspoon ground ginger

Chop off the wing tips; discard them, or save them for making soup. Cut each wing into 2 pieces. Place the wings in a glass baking dish. Combine the remaining ingredients and pour this mixture over the wings. Marinate overnight in the refrigerator. Preheat the oven to 350 degrees. Remove the chicken wings from the marinade and place them in a shallow pan (a jelly-roll pan is perfect). Pour 1 cup marinade liquid over. Bake for 1 hour.

Spinach and Shrimp Dip

YIELDS 5 CUPS

1½–2 cups fresh peeled shrimp
1 pound cream cheese, at room
   temperature
1½ cups heavy cream
5 tablespoons butter
4 cloves garlic, minced
1½ cups shredded Monterey Jack
   cheese

1 tablespoon lemon pepper
1 tablespoon fresh lemon juice
1 teaspoon paprika
Salt and pepper
Two 10-ounce packages frozen
   chopped spinach, thawed

Drop the shrimp into a pot of boiling water and cook just until the shrimp turn pink, 2 to 3 minutes. Let cool and chop. Set aside. In a heavy saucepan, over low heat, mix together the cream cheese, heavy cream, 4 tablespoons of the butter, and garlic. Cook, stirring, until the cream cheese is melted. Add the Jack cheese, lemon pepper, lemon juice, paprika, and salt and pepper to taste, and stir until cheese is melted. Melt the remaining tablespoon of butter in another saucepan. Squeeze out any water remaining in the thawed spinach. Add the spinach and cook, 2 to 3 minutes. Drain the spinach and add it to the cream cheese mixture. Stir and simmer for 5 to 8 minutes. Add the shrimp. Serve the dip in a chafing dish along with toast points or French bread for dipping. ❦ ❦ ❦ **The Lady & Sons**

Italian Chicken Sticks

YIELDS ABOUT 3–3½ DOZEN

1 cup seasoned breadcrumbs
½ cup freshly grated Parmesan
1½ teaspoons dried thyme
1½ teaspoons dried basil
1 teaspoon dried oregano
½ teaspoon salt
¼ teaspoon garlic powder

Pinch of ground red pepper
8 boneless chicken breast halves,
*   cut into ½-inch strips*
½ cup (1 stick) melted butter
Marinara sauce or honey mustard
*   for dipping*

Preheat the oven to 400 degrees. In a pie plate or platter, combine the breadcrumbs, Parmesan, thyme, basil, oregano, salt, garlic powder, and red pepper. Dip the chicken strips in the melted butter, then dredge them in the breadcrumb mixture. Place the chicken strips in a single layer on a lightly greased baking sheet. Bake for 20 minutes, or until the chicken is cooked through. Serve the chicken sticks hot with marinara sauce, or serve hot or cold with honey mustard.

Shore Is Good Seafood Dip

YIELDS 4 CUPS

2 tablespoons butter
1 medium green bell pepper, diced
1 medium onion, diced
2 stalks celery, diced
Half of a 10¾-ounce can cream of
 shrimp soup (discard top half
 and use bottom part of soup)

1 cup mayonnaise
½ pound freshly grated Parmesan
6-ounce can crabmeat, picked free
 of any broken shells, drained
6 ounces shrimp, fresh or canned,
 drained
½ teaspoon white pepper

Preheat oven to 325 degrees. Melt the butter in a skillet over medium heat. Add the bell pepper, onion, and celery, and sauté for 2 minutes. In a bowl, combine the soup, mayonnaise, Parmesan, crabmeat, shrimp, and pepper. Stir the sautéed vegetables into the seafood mixture and spoon this mixture into a lightly greased 8 × 11-inch casserole dish. Bake for 30 minutes. Serve with toast points or crackers.

Sugar-and-Nut-Glazed Brie

SERVES 16–20

¼ cup packed brown sugar
¼ cup chopped macadamia nuts
 or pecans
1 tablespoon brandy
One 14-ounce round of Brie

Apple wedges
Pear wedges
Lemon juice
Crackers

In a small bowl stir together the sugar, nuts, and brandy. Cover and chill for at least 24 hours or up to one week. At serving time, place the Brie on an ovenproof platter or pie plate. Bake at 500 degrees for 4 or 5 minutes or until the Brie is slightly softened. Spread the sugar mixture in an even layer on top of the warm Brie, and bake for 2 to 3 minutes longer, or until the sugar melts. Brush the fruit wedges with lemon juice and arrange them around one side of the Brie. Place crackers around the other side.

Tomato Canapés

YIELDS 15 CANAPÉS

¾ cup finely diced tomatoes
2 teaspoons finely diced onions
1 teaspoon finely chopped fresh
    basil
⅛ teaspoon The Lady's House
    Seasoning
One 2.1-ounce package Athens

brand mini phyllo shells
½ cup packed shredded mozzarella
¼ cup mayonnaise
2 tablespoons Hormel Real Bacon
    pieces, or more as needed

Preheat the oven to 350 degrees. Place the diced tomatoes in a colander. Sprinkle with the onions, basil, and House Seasoning, and toss to coat. Allow to drain, stirring occasionally.

Fill each phyllo shell with 1 teaspoon of the tomato mixture. Stir together the mozzarella and mayonnaise. Frost the top of each shell with 1 teaspoon of the mayonnaise mixture. Sprinkle each shell with ¼ teaspoon of bacon pieces. Bake the filled shells for 10 to 12 minutes. Serve hot. These may be prepared ahead of time and refrigerated until serving time.

Mushroom Canapés

YIELDS 15 CANAPÉS

1 cup mayonnaise
½ cup freshly grated Parmesan
One 4-ounce can mushroom pieces
    and stems, drained
One 2.8-ounce can french-fried
    onion rings

One 12-ounce loaf of Pepperidge
    Farm party rye or
    pumpernickel

In a bowl, stir together the mayonnaise, Parmesan, mushrooms, and onion rings. Spread on lightly toasted party rye or pumpernickel. Place the canapés on a baking sheet and broil until the topping is bubbly.

ℐrtichoke Frittata

SERVES 8–10

Two 6-ounce jars marinated
   artichoke hearts
1 small onion, finely chopped
1 clove garlic, minced or mashed
4 eggs, lightly beaten
¼ cup fine breadcrumbs

¼ teaspoon salt
⅛ teaspoon each pepper, oregano,
   and hot sauce
½ pound (2 cups) shredded
   Cheddar cheese
2 tablespoons minced fresh parsley

Preheat the oven to 325 degrees. Drain the artichoke marinade into a large skillet. Chop the drained artichokes and set aside. Heat the marinade over medium heat, add the onion and garlic, and sauté for 5 minutes. Place the beaten eggs in a large bowl. Add the breadcrumbs, salt, pepper, oregano, and hot sauce to the eggs, then stir in the cheese. Add the chopped artichokes and the sautéed onion and garlic, along with the liquid in the skillet. Pour the mixture into a greased 7 × 11-inch pan. Bake for 30 minutes, or until set. To serve, cut into squares. The frittata may be served hot or cold, and may be frozen after baking. Reheat in a 300-degree oven for 10 minutes. Double or triple the recipe, using 2 or 3 pans, for a big party.

Chicken Nuggets

SERVES 12

2 cups crushed sour-cream-and-
   onion-flavored potato chips
1 egg
2 tablespoons milk

6 chicken breast fillets, cut into
   1½-inch cubes
⅓ cup butter

Preheat the oven to 350 degrees. Spread the crushed potato chips in a shallow dish. Beat together the egg and milk in a shallow bowl. Dip the chicken cubes into the egg mixture and then dredge them in the chips. Place the chicken nuggets on a baking sheet and drizzle with melted butter. Bake for 15 to 18 minutes, or until golden brown. The chicken nuggets can be frozen after baking. Serve with your favorite sauce, such as honey mustard or ranch dressing.

Black Bean Dip

SERVES 6–8

2 tablespoons butter
2 tablespoons chopped onion
One 4-ounce can green chilies, chopped
1 tomato, diced
2 teaspoons chopped fresh cilantro (optional)
1 teaspoon The Lady's House Seasoning

One 15-ounce can black beans with jalapeños
1 cup shredded Cheddar cheese
4-ounce block Velveeta Mexican cheese product, diced
1 3-ounce package cream cheese, diced

Melt the butter in a skillet. Add the onions and sauté until tender, about 5 minutes. Add the green chilies, tomato, cilantro, and House Seasoning, and cook for 5 minutes longer. Add the beans and cheeses, and simmer until hot and bubbling. Serve hot with white-corn tortilla chips.

Shrimp Mold

SERVES 12–15

The juice from one 6½-ounce can minced clams, clams reserved for another use
Three ¼-ounce packets unflavored gelatin
1 pound fresh shrimp, cooked
One 8-ounce package cream cheese
1 small onion, grated

1 cup mayonnaise
1 cup chopped celery
1 tablespoon Worcestershire sauce
The Lady's Insane Salt
Fresh chopped parsley and paprika, for garnish

Place the clam juice in a large bowl. Add the gelatin and stir until dissolved. Add the shrimp, cream cheese, onion, mayonnaise, celery, Worcestershire sauce, and Insane Salt to taste. Pour the mixture into a lightly greased 1-quart mold and refrigerate for at least 2 hours or until firm. To serve, turn the mold out onto a platter. Garnish with parsley and paprika. Serve with crackers.

South Georgia "Caviar"

SERVES 15

*Two 15-ounce cans black-eyed
   peas, drained*
*One 15-ounce can whole kernel
   corn, drained*
*One 10-ounce can Ro-Tel
   tomatoes*
2 cups chopped red bell pepper

*½ cup chopped fresh jalapeño
   peppers*
½ cup chopped onion
*One 8-ounce bottle Italian salad
   dressing*
*One 4-ounce jar chopped pimentos,
   drained*

Combine all the ingredients in a large bowl, stir gently to combine, and refrigerate overnight. Serve with corn chips. This recipe will keep in the refrigerator for up to 2 weeks.

Devilish Cheese Logs

SERVES 12

*1 cup shredded sharp Cheddar
   cheese, at room temperature*
*One 8-ounce package cream
   cheese, at room temperature*

One 4½-ounce can deviled ham
½ cup chopped pitted green olives
½ cup finely chopped pecans

In a small bowl, blend together the Cheddar and cream cheeses. Beat in the deviled ham, then stir in the olives.

Refrigerate the mixture for at least 2 hours so it's firm enough to slice.

Shape the cheese mixture into two 8-inch logs. Roll the cheese logs in chopped nuts. Serve with crackers.

Georgia Spiced Pecans

YIELDS 2½ CUPS

1 cup sugar
½ teaspoon cinnamon
⅓ cup evaporated milk

2 cups pecan halves
1 teaspoon vanilla extract

Combine the sugar, cinnamon, and milk in a medium-size saucepan. Bring to a boil and cook to the soft-ball stage (234–238 degrees on a candy thermometer). Add the pecans and vanilla and stir well. Using a slotted spoon, drop single pecans on a sheet of waxed paper; allow to cool.

Tangy Marinated Shrimp

YIELDS 26–30 SHRIMP

The marinade in this recipe also makes a wonderful salad dressing.

4 tablespoons olive oil
2 tablespoons white vinegar
1 teaspoon The Lady's House Seasoning
⅔ cup mayonnaise
2 scant tablespoons anchovy paste
2 tablespoons Creole or brown mustard

1 pound large cooked shrimp, peeled, with tails left on
1 red bell pepper, sliced into thin strips
4 green onions, chopped, using entire onion
2 tablespoons chopped fresh parsley
1 tablespoon fresh lemon juice

In a glass or ceramic bowl, beat together the oil, vinegar, and House Seasoning. Add the mayonnaise, anchovy paste, and mustard, and stir until well blended. Fold in the shrimp, bell pepper, onion, parsley, and lemon juice. Marinate overnight in the refrigerator. Serve cold or at room temperature.

Caviar Spread

YIELDS 3 CUPS

3 hard-boiled eggs
Salt and pepper
1 medium cucumber
Two 4-ounce jars caviar
One 8-ounce package cream cheese

1 small bunch green onions, finely sliced
¾ cup mayonnaise
Green onions, chopped, for garnish

Finely chop the eggs; season with salt and pepper to taste. Peel, seed and chop the cucumber. Blot with paper towels to remove excess moisture. Reserve ½ cup of caviar for the garnish.

In an 8-inch round serving dish, layer the ingredients in the following order: cream cheese, caviar, eggs, sliced green onions, cucumber, and mayonnaise. Garnish with chopped green onions and the reserved caviar; you can make a pretty pattern with the caviar. Serve with crackers.

Candied Dills

YIELDS 1 QUART

1 quart whole dill pickles
2¾ cups sugar

½ cup tarragon vinegar
2 tablespoons pickling spice

Drain the pickles, cut into ½-inch slices, and place them in a deep glass or ceramic bowl. Add the sugar and vinegar. Place the pickling spices in a small square of cheesecloth, tie it closed, and add to the bowl. Let stand at room temperature until the sugar is dissolved, about 4 hours. Pour the pickles into a 1-quart jar, cover, and refrigerate. These pickles taste best after 2 or 3 days. Remove the spice bag after one week.

"Boursin Cheese"

YIELDS 3 CUPS

The Boursin cheese sold in the grocery store is kind of on the pricey side, so just make your own and enjoy the savings.

1 pound cream cheese
8 ounces whipped butter, at room
   temperature
1 teaspoon garlic salt
½ teaspoon dried oregano

¼ teaspoon dried basil
¼ teaspoon dried dill
¼ teaspoon dried marjoram
¼ teaspoon black pepper
¼ teaspoon dried thyme

Place the cream cheese and butter in the bowl of a food processor. With the machine running, add the seasonings, and process until smoothly blended. Line a medium-size crock or bowl with plastic wrap and fill it with the cheese mixture. Cover and refrigerate for up to 1 week. Serve with buttery crackers. This also makes a tasty spread for roast beef sandwiches.   🌿 🌿 🌿   ***The Lady & Sons***

Herbed Cheese-and-Cracker Bits

SERVES 18–20

Two 10½-ounce boxes Ritz Cheese
   Bits (not peanut butter flavor)
½ cup vegetable oil
One 1-ounce package Hidden
   Valley Original Ranch salad
   dressing mix

1 heaping tablespoon dried dill
1 teaspoon garlic powder
1 teaspoon celery salt

Place the crackers in a large sealable freezer container. In a bowl, mix the oil, salad dressing mix, dill, garlic powder, and celery salt. Pour this mixture over the crackers, cover the container, and invert it to coat the crackers with seasoning. Refrigerate for at least 24 hours, turning the container every so often to keep the crackers coated. Let the mixture come to room temperature before serving. Store in the covered container in the refrigerator.

Party Eye-of-Round Steak

YIELDS 14–18

½ cup vegetable oil
½ cup bourbon
One 0.7-ounce package Italian
   salad dressing mix

2–3-pound eye-of-round beef steak
Salt
Coarsely ground black pepper

In a shallow glass dish, combine the oil, bourbon, and salad dressing mix. Add the beef and turn to coat it with the marinade. Cover and refrigerate overnight.

Preheat the oven to 325 degrees. Remove the meat from the marinade and blot it dry with a paper towel. Salt the meat, then coat it heavily with pepper. Roast uncovered until a meat thermometer registers your preferred doneness. Cool the beef, slice thin, and serve with assorted breads and spreads, including a variety of mustards.

Mexican Layered Dip

SERVES 20

3 ripe avocados, peeled and
   mashed
2 tablespoons fresh lemon juice
Pinch of garlic salt
Pinch of black pepper
Dash of hot sauce
1 cup sour cream
1 cup mayonnaise
One 1¼-ounce package taco
   seasoning
Four 9-ounce cans Frito-Lay bean
   dip
One 16-ounce jar picante sauce or
   drained salsa (optional)

1 cup chopped onion or green
   onions
3 tomatoes, chopped
One 6-ounce can pitted black
   olives, drained
Sliced jalapeño peppers (optional)
8 ounces sharp Cheddar cheese,
   grated
4 ounces Monterey Jack cheese,
   grated

In a bowl, stir together the avocado, lemon juice, garlic salt, black pepper, and hot sauce; set aside. In another bowl, mix the sour cream, mayonnaise, and taco seasoning; set aside. In a wide, shallow bowl, layer the bean dip, avocado mixture, sour-cream mixture, picante sauce, onions, tomatoes, olives, and jalapeño peppers to taste, and top with both cheeses. Serve with tortilla chips.

Salsa Chicken Salad

SERVES 4

1 pint sour cream
One 16-ounce jar chunky salsa
Half of a 1-ounce package
  Hidden Valley Original Ranch
  salad dressing mix
2 cups diced cooked chicken breast
  or two 8-ounce cans premium
  white-meat chicken

One 8-ounce can sliced water
  chestnuts, drained
1 cup shredded pepper Jack cheese

In a large bowl, stir together the sour cream, salsa, and salad dressing mix. Fold in the chicken, water chestnuts, and cheese. Refrigerate until well chilled. Serve with chips, crackers, or flour tortillas.

Smoked Oyster Cheese Balls

SERVES 12

Two 8-ounce packages cream
cheese, at room temperature
One 3 ¾-ounce can smoked oysters,
drained
One 0.4-ounce package Hidden
Valley Original Ranch
Buttermilk Recipe salad
dressing mix
1 tablespoon fresh lemon juice
1 heaping tablespoon Durkee
Famous Sauce

COATING OPTIONS
Cracked black pepper
Chopped green onions
Cracker crumbs
Bacon bits
Chopped pecans
Chopped fresh parsley

In a large bowl, mix the cream cheese, oysters, salad dressing mix, lemon juice, and Durkee Famous Sauce with a fork. Refrigerate the mixture until workable, about 30 minutes. Place the cheese mixture on a sheet of waxed paper and shape into ball. Roll the ball in one or more of the suggested coatings (or create your own). I like to coat the cheese ball with cracked pepper (2 tablespoons) and then with chopped green onions (½–¾ cup).

Zesty Cheese Straws

YIELDS 5 DOZEN

½ cup (1 stick) butter, at room
temperature
1 pound sharp Cheddar cheese,
shredded, at room temperature

2 cups all-purpose flour
1 teaspoon salt
¼ teaspoon ground red pepper

Preheat the oven to 300 degrees. In a mixing bowl, cream the butter until light and fluffy. Add the cheese and mix until blended. Add the flour, salt, and red pepper, and mix to form a dough. Refrigerate for 30 minutes to firm up the dough, then place it in a cookie press, fitted with a ridged tip. Pipe the dough in 2-inch strips onto a lightly greased cookie sheet. Bake for 10 to 15 minutes, or until lightly browned. Remove to racks to cool.

Stuffed French Bread

SERVES 12–15

3 small loaves French bread,
    approximately 6 inches long
Two 8-ounce packages cream
    cheese, at room temperature
1 cup mayonnaise
One 2-ounce jar pimento,
    drained and chopped

⅓ cup chopped fresh parsley
One 0.7-ounce package Italian
    salad dressing mix
One 2.25-ounce jar of chopped
    dried beef (optional)

Cut each loaf in half lengthwise to stuff. Remove some of the inside of the bread to make room for the stuffing. Combine the remaining ingredients and mix well. Fill the hollows in the bread with the mixture. Reassemble the bread into loaves. Wrap in plastic wrap and refrigerate until ready to serve, at least 3 hours. To serve, slice the loaves into 1-inch sections.

Egg Caviar Mold

SERVES 4–6

4 hard-boiled eggs
5 tablespoons butter, at room
    temperature
⅓ cup chopped green onions

⅓ cup mayonnaise
½ teaspoon fresh lemon juice
¼ cup sour cream
One 3.5-ounce jar caviar

In the bowl of a food processor, combine the eggs, butter, onions, mayonnaise, and lemon juice, and process until well blended. Fill a small greased mold with this mixture and refrigerate for at least 3 hours. Turn the mold out onto a platter. Spread sour cream over and then sprinkle caviar on top. Serve with butter crackers or toast points.

Soups and Salads

SOUPS

The Lady & Sons Beef Vegetable Soup

Poblano Chicken Chowder

Dian's Black Bean Soup

Vegetable Cheese Soup

Michele's Chicken Noodle Soup

Chef Jack's Corn Chowder

Susan's Caldo Soup

The Lady & Sons Crab Stew

Crab Bisque

Potato and Ham Soup

Senate Bean Soup

Chilled Zucchini Soup

BLT Soup

Mushroom Cloud Soup

Wayne's Award-Winning Maryland Crab Soup

Bean and Bacon Soup

Taco Soup

Homemade Dried Onion Soup Mix

SALADS

Hawaiian Chicken Salad

Nancy's Cole Slaw

Pecan Cranberry Salad

Golda's Frozen Waldorf Salad

Feta Cheese and Tomato Salad

Chinese Salad

Gingersnap Pear Salad

Pickled Beets and Eggs

Spinach, Strawberry, and Hearts of Palm Salad

Blueberry Salad

Marinated Asparagus Salad

Fettuccine Chicken Salad

Colo Cucumber Salad

Thanksgiving Apple Salad

Fruit Salad with Honey Dressing

My Mother's Congealed Salad

Copper Pennies

Strawberry Mold

Fruit Bowl

Warm Apple and Goat Cheese Salad

Cherry Tomato and Mushroom Salad

Strawberry Pretzel Salad

Marinated Shrimp and Artichoke Hearts

The Lady & Sons Beef Vegetable Soup

YIELDS 8 QUARTS

Don't let the lengthy ingredient list scare you away. It's really not as bad as it looks. Even my brother, Bubba, can make it. On a cold winter's day it will make your tongue want to slap your brains out! This recipe serves two or three dozen people, but can easily be cut in half. It keeps for up to five days in the refrigerator or two months in the freezer.

2½–3 pounds beef short ribs or 2½–3-pound boneless chuck roast*

2 tablespoons vegetable oil (if using chuck roast)

4 quarts cold water

1 tablespoon dried Italian seasoning

3 tablespoons dried parsley

1 teaspoon garlic powder

1 tablespoon beef bouillon granules

1 tablespoon The Lady's House Seasoning

1 tablespoon The Lady's Seasoned Salt

2 bay leaves

½ teaspoon black pepper

1 teaspoon celery salt

1 tablespoon Worcestershire sauce

1½ cups chopped onion

One 28-ounce can diced tomatoes

1 cup thinly sliced carrots

1 cup diced celery

1 cup sliced green beans, fresh or canned

1 cup frozen black-eyed peas

1 cup frozen butter beans

1 cup cut okra, fresh or frozen

1 cup corn kernels, fresh or canned

1 cup diced potatoes

½ cup uncooked elbow macaroni

2 teaspoons Accent (optional)

If using chuck roast, heat the oil in a large skillet over medium heat. Place the roast in the skillet and cook until browned on both sides, about 5 minutes per side. Remove the roast from the skillet and cut it into 1½ to 2-inch cubes; discard the fat. Place the beef cubes in a large stockpot. (If using short ribs, you can put them right in the pot with no preparation.) Add the water, seasonings, onion, and tomatoes and bring to a boil over high heat. Cover the pot, reduce the heat so that the liquid simmers, and cook for 1½ to 2 hours, or until the meat is very

*The chuck roast will yield more meat, but the bones from the short ribs give the soup an incredible flavor.

tender. If using short ribs, remove them from the pot and cut the meat from the bones, discard the bones and fat, and return the meat to the pot. Add the remaining vegetables and the macaroni, and return the soup to a boil, stirring to distribute the ingredients. Reduce the heat and simmer for 45 minutes. Add Accent, if desired, and adjust the other seasonings to taste. To remove excess fat from the surface of the soup, swirl a lettuce leaf around the surface—it will pick up a lot of the fat.

❦ ❦ ❦ *The Lady & Sons*

Poblano Chicken Chowder

SERVES 12–16

¼ cup olive oil

3 large carrots, cut into ½-inch dice

2 large onions, cut into ½-inch dice

5 stalks celery, cut into ½-inch pieces

⅛ cup minced garlic

2–3 small poblano peppers, seeded and cut into ½-inch dice

1 teaspoon salt

½ teaspoon white pepper

¼ teaspoon cumin, or more to taste

¼ teaspoon dried thyme, or more to taste

1 tablespoon chicken bouillon granules

3 quarts chicken broth

½ bunch fresh cilantro, minced

3 cups diced (large pieces) grilled chicken

½ cup (1 stick) unsalted butter

1 cup all-purpose flour

½ teaspoon hot sauce, or more to taste

1 cup heavy cream

Heat the oil in a large stockpot over medium heat. Add the carrots, onions, celery, garlic, poblano peppers, salt, white pepper, cumin, and thyme. Sauté for 7 to 8 minutes, or until the vegetables begin to soften. Stir in the chicken bouillon. Add the chicken broth and cilantro, and cook for 10 to 12 minutes, or until the carrots are tender. Stir in the chicken and cook, stirring frequently, until the chowder is thick and the chicken is heated through. Shortly before the chowder is done, melt the butter in a large skillet over medium heat. Add the flour and stir to combine. Cook, stirring frequently, for 3 to 4 minutes to cook the flour. Do not allow the mixture to brown! Ladle 1 cup of the hot liquid from the stockpot into the skillet, whisking constantly.

When the first cup of liquid is incorporated, add another 2 cups of liquid, one at a time. Pour the mixture in the skillet into the stockpot, whisking to blend. Cook, stirring frequently, for 3 to 5 minutes longer, or until the mixture begins to thicken. Remove the pot from the heat. Stir in the hot sauce, then the cream, and serve.

Dian's Black Bean Soup

SERVES 12

1 pound dry black beans	*Two 14½-ounce cans chicken broth*
1 tablespoon vegetable oil	*4 cups water*
2 cups chopped onions	*¼ teaspoon dried thyme*
1 cup finely chopped carrots	*One 14½-ounce can Del Monte*
1 cup finely chopped celery	*Mexican tomatoes*
2 tablespoons minced garlic	*1½ teaspoons salt*
2 teaspoons cumin	*Sour cream*
¼–½ teaspoon red pepper flakes	*Chopped green onions*
1 pound smoked ham hocks	*Finely chopped crisp bacon*

Place the beans in a large pot and add water to cover by 2 inches. Soak the beans overnight.

Drain the soaking liquid from the beans. Heat the oil in a Dutch oven over medium heat and add the onions, carrots, and celery; cook, stirring occasionally, until tender. Add the garlic, cumin, and pepper flakes, and cook for 30 seconds longer. Add the ham hocks, then stir in the beans, chicken broth, water, and thyme. Bring to a boil, reduce the heat, cover, and simmer for 1 hour. Stir in the tomatoes with their liquid, and the salt. Simmer, covered, until the beans are very tender, 1 to 2 hours longer. Remove the ham hock and cut the meat from the bones. Discard the skin and bones and return the meat to the pot. With a potato masher, mash some of the solids in the soup to thicken the broth. Ladle the soup into bowls and serve with a dollop of sour cream on top. Sprinkle with onions and bacon. ❦ ❦ ❦ ***The Lady & Sons***

Vegetable Cheese Soup

SERVES 8–10

1 cup diced celery
1 cup diced onion
4 chicken bouillon cubes
4 cups water
3 cups cubed potatoes
1 cup shredded carrots
One 10-ounce package frozen
creamed corn

One 10-ounce package frozen
mixed vegetables
One 10¾-ounce can cream of
chicken soup
1½-pound block Velveeta cheese
product, cubed
Salt and pepper

In a large saucepan, bring the water to a boil, and add the celery, onion, and bouillon cubes. Reduce to medium heat. Cook for 20 minutes. Add the potatoes, carrots, corn, mixed vegetables, and soup, and cook until the vegetables are tender. Reduce the heat to low and add the cheese. Cook, stirring gently, until the cheese has melted and the soup is hot; do not boil. Add salt and pepper to taste.

Michele's Chicken Noodle Soup

SERVES 6–8

One whole 3–4 pound chicken with
skin and fat removed
3 quarts water
3 onions, quartered
3 carrots, quartered
3 stalks celery, halved
6 whole dried Chinese black
mushrooms (optional)

2 cloves garlic
4 sprigs fresh parsley
2 bay leaves
2 teaspoons salt
¼ teaspoon black pepper
5–7 ounces of your favorite egg
noodles (I prefer dumpling
style)

Place the chicken in a large stockpot. Add the water and place over medium-high heat. Add the vegetables, mushrooms (if using), garlic, parsley, bay leaves, salt, and pepper. Bring to a boil, reduce the heat, and simmer, partially covered, for 1½ hours. Remove the chicken from the pot. Remove the meat from the bones and cut into bite-size pieces; set aside. Remove the mushrooms, if using, and set aside. Remove and discard the bay leaves. With a slotted spoon, remove the rest of the solids from the stockpot and transfer them to a blender or large food processor. Purée the solids, adding some of the liquid from the stockpot if it is too thick to blend; set aside. Return the remaining stock to a boil, add the noodles, and cook until al dente—tender but still slightly firm. Reduce the heat, stir in the puréed vegetables, chicken, and mushrooms, and serve.

Chef Jack's Corn Chowder

SERVES 8–10

1 cup (2 sticks) butter
1 small onion, diced
1 small carrot, finely diced
1 small celery stalk, diced
1 clove garlic, minced
½ cup all-purpose flour

3 cups white corn kernels, fresh or
   frozen
3 cups chicken stock
2 cups half-and-half
Pinch of freshly grated nutmeg
Salt and pepper

Melt 1 stick of butter in a large skillet over medium heat. Add the onion, carrot, celery, and garlic, and sauté for 2 minutes. Add the flour and stir to make a roux. Cook until the roux is lightly browned; set aside to cool to room temperature. Meanwhile, combine the corn and chicken stock in a saucepan, and bring to a boil. Simmer for 10 minutes. Pour the boiling stock with the corn (a little at a time) into the skillet with the roux, whisking briskly so it doesn't lump. Return the skillet to the heat and bring to a boil. The mixture should become very thick. In a small saucepan, gently heat the half-and-half; stir it into the thick corn mixture. Add the nutmeg and salt and pepper to taste. Just before serving, cut the remaining stick of butter into large chunks. Add it to enrich the soup, stirring until the butter melts.

❧ ❧ ❧ **The Lady & Sons**

Susan's Caldo Soup

SERVES 4–6

½ pound Hillshire Farm Smoked
   Sausage
2 tablespoons butter
½ cup diced onion
Three 14½-ounce cans chicken
   broth

5 small new red potatoes,
   quartered
1 teaspoon The Lady's House
   Seasoning
One 10-ounce package frozen
   chopped collard greens

Cut the sausage into ¼-inch slices. Melt the butter over medium heat in a large saucepan; add the onion and sausage, and sauté until the onion is transparent, about 10 minutes. Add the chicken broth, potatoes, and House Seasoning. Bring to a boil, reduce the heat, cover, and cook for 10 minutes. Add the collard greens, cover, and cook for 20 minutes longer. Before serving, using a fork, mash some of the potatoes to thicken the soup.   ❦ ❦ ❦   **The Lady & Sons**

The Lady & Sons Crab Stew

SERVES 10–12

4 tablespoons butter
3 tablespoons all-purpose flour
1 tablespoon minced garlic
2 cups heavy cream
2 cups half-and-half
2 Knorr fish-flavor bouillon cubes
1 pound crabmeat, picked free of
   any broken shells

¼ cup sherry
½ teaspoon white pepper
One 8-ounce bottle clam juice
   (optional)
Grated Parmesan and snipped
   chives, for garnish

Heat the butter in a large saucepan over medium heat. Add the flour, stirring to blend it in, then add the garlic. Gradually add the cream and half-and-half, stirring constantly. Add the bouillon cubes and stir well. As the mixture begins to thicken, add the crabmeat, then the sherry and pepper. If the stew seems too thick, thin it with clam juice, which will also add a lot of flavor. Serve in a mug, garnished with grated Parmesan and snipped chives.

❀ ❀ ❀ **The Lady & Sons**

Crab Bisque

SERVES 4

One 10¾-ounce can cream of
   asparagus soup
One 10¾-ounce can cream of
   mushroom soup
¼ cup milk

¼ cup half-and-half
½ pound crabmeat, picked free of
   any broken shells
¼ cup dry sherry

Combine all the ingredients in a heavy saucepan and bring to a boil. Reduce the heat and simmer for 5 minutes.

This delicate tasting soup can be frozen for up to 1 month.

Potato and Ham Soup

SERVES 10–12

5 pounds Russet baking potatoes,
   cut into 1-inch cubes
1 thick slice of cooked ham, cut
   into small pieces (not country
   ham, which is too salty)

½ cup (1 stick) butter
Salt and pepper
1 cup half-and-half
½ cup sour cream

Place the potatoes in a large pot and add enough water to just cover the potatoes (too much water will make the soup too thin). Cover and bring to a boil, then uncover and cook over medium-high heat for 20 minutes. Reduce the heat and add the ham and butter. Season with salt and pepper to taste. Over low heat, add the half-and-half and sour cream; keep warm over low heat until serving time. I promise that everyone will want the recipe (men more than women)!

❀ ❀ ❀ **The Lady & Sons**

Senate Bean Soup

SERVES 12

Years ago, Mrs. Herman Talmadge, wife of our state senator, shared with us Georgia ladies the bean soup recipe that was served in the Senate dining room. It is quite wonderful.

2 pounds Michigan navy beans	*¼ cup (½ stick) butter*
4 quarts water	*1 medium onion, chopped*
1½ pounds smoked ham hocks	*Salt and pepper*

Rinse the beans in hot water until they are white. Place them in a stockpot, add the water, and bring to a boil. Reduce the heat and simmer for 3 hours. Meanwhile, simmer the ham hocks in a large pot of water for 3 hours. Heat the butter in a small skillet over medium heat. Sauté the onion until lightly browned. Add the onion to the pot of beans. Remove two cups of the bean mixture, purée in a blender, and return to the soup. Remove the ham hocks, and break down slightly with a knife. Add to soup mixture. Just before serving, season the soup with salt and pepper to taste. ❦ ❦ ❦ **The Lady & Sons**

Chilled Zucchini Soup

SERVES 4

2 cups chicken broth	*1 cup mayonnaise*
2 large onions, chopped	*1 teaspoon fresh lemon juice*
3 medium zucchini, sliced	*Half-and-half (optional)*
1 clove garlic, sliced	*Lemon slices*
¼ teaspoon salt	

Combine the broth, onions, zucchini, garlic, and salt in a large saucepan and bring to a boil. Cook the vegetables for 5 to 8 minutes, or until tender. Let cool to room temperature, then transfer the mixture to a food processor, add the mayonnaise and lemon juice, and process until smooth. Refrigerate over-night. Thin with a little half-and-half if necessary. Serve cold, with lemon slices.

BLT Soup

SERVES 8

5 slices bacon, diced small
½ cup diced green onions
2 tablespoons butter
3½ cups iceberg lettuce, julienned
½ cup instant-blending flour
3½ cups fresh or canned chicken
   broth, heated to a simmer

1 cup diced fresh tomatoes
⅛ teaspoon grated fresh nutmeg
⅛ teaspoon ground red pepper
1 cup heavy cream
¼ cup mayonnaise
¼ cup sour cream
Crisp crumbled bacon

In a 3-quart pot, cook the bacon over medium heat till lightly browned. Add the onions and cook, stirring, until wilted. Add the butter and stir until melted. Add the lettuce and sauté for 2 minutes. Sprinkle the flour into the pot, then stir it in until well blended. Remove the pot from the heat and add the hot chicken broth, tomatoes, nutmeg, and pepper. Heat the soup to boiling, stirring constantly, then reduce the heat and simmer gently for 5 minutes. Add the cream and mix well. Mix together the mayonnaise and sour cream. Serve each portion of soup with a dollop of the mayonnaise mixture topped with crumbled bacon.   ❧ ❧ ❧ **The Lady & Sons**

Mushroom Cloud Soup

SERVES 4

This is the perfect soup if you don't have much time. The whole thing's made in the microwave, and it's delicious.

¼ cup (½ stick) butter
½ pound sliced mushrooms
1 medium onion, chopped
1 cup lightly packed chopped fresh
   parsley

1 tablespoon all-purpose flour
One 14-ounce can beef broth
1 cup sour cream
Mushroom slices

In a 7 × 11-inch baking dish, heat the butter for 30 seconds in the microwave to melt it. Add the mushrooms, onion, and parsley, and microwave for 5 minutes, stirring once or twice. Stir in the flour and ½ cup of the beef broth. Cook, uncovered, for 1 to 2 minutes, or until bubbly. In a blender, working in batches, purée the mixture with the sour cream and the remaining beef broth. Return the soup to the baking dish and reheat for 3 minutes. If the soup is made ahead, cover and refrigerate. Serve cold, or reheat the soup, covered, in the microwave for 3 minutes. Ladle the soup into bowls and float mushroom slices on top.

Wayne's Award-Winning Maryland Crab Soup

YIELDS ABOUT 8 QUARTS

I've often spoken of all the interesting and wonderful people who cross my path. Well, Wayne Brokke is one of those people. Wayne had seen me on QVC several times, and when the opportunity arose for a trip to Savannah, he made a special point of coming in to meet me. We had a great time getting to know each other. Wayne is the owner of Wayne's Bar-B-Que in Baltimore, where he also does cooking segments for a local television station. When I mentioned to Wayne that I was writing another cookbook, he graciously offered to share a few of his recipes. They are Wayne's Cranberry Sauce, and the following recipe, which is a five-time winner of the Maryland Old Bay Soupstakes Critics and People's Choice Award. Thanks, Wayne, and continued good luck to you!

4 quarts water
2 tablespoons chicken bouillon
   granules
2 tablespoons beef bouillon
   granules
6 soup crabs, or three small live
   crabs, cleaned and rinsed
3 cups canned crushed tomatoes
¼ cup Worcestershire sauce
2 tablespoons Old Bay Seasoning,
   or more to taste
2 tablespoons sugar
1 teaspoon Tabasco sauce
2 bay leaves

1½ cups sliced carrots
1½ cups chopped celery
1½ cups corn kernels, fresh or
   frozen
1½ cups green beans, fresh or frozen
1½ cups lima beans, fresh or frozen
1 cup chopped cabbage
1 medium onion, chopped
2 cups cubed red potatoes, skins on
1 pound lump crabmeat, picked
   free of any broken shells
1 pound claw crabmeat, picked
   free of any broken shells
Salt and pepper

Bring the water to a boil in a stockpot, then add the chicken and beef bouillon granules and stir until dissolved. Cut the whole crabs in half, add them to the pot, and bring to a second boil. Skim any excess froth created by the crab parts. Add the tomatoes, Worcestershire sauce, Old Bay Seasoning, sugar, Tabasco, and bay leaves, and stir to combine. Add the carrots, celery, corn, green beans, lima beans, cabbage, and onion, bring to a low boil, and cook for 10 minutes. Add the potatoes and cook until tender. Add the crabmeat and cook for 10 minutes. Season with salt and pepper to taste.

Bean and Bacon Soup

SERVES 4

1 cup dry navy beans	*½ teaspoon paprika*
6 slices bacon	*2½ cups chicken broth*
1 carrot, diced	*One 16-ounce can crushed tomatoes*
1 red bell pepper, diced	*1 bay leaf*
1 small onion, chopped	*The Lady's House Seasoning*
1 large clove garlic, minced	*Crumbled bacon*

To quick-soak the beans, place them in a pot and add 2 cups of water. Bring to a boil, cover, and boil for 1 minute. Remove the pot from the heat and let the beans stand in the hot water for 1 hour. Meanwhile, fry the bacon in a Dutch oven until crisp. Remove the bacon and set aside. Add the carrot and bell pepper to the Dutch oven and sauté for 5 minutes. Add the onion and garlic and sauté for 5 minutes longer. Stir in the paprika. Cook, stirring, for a few minutes longer to develop the flavor of the paprika. Slowly add the chicken broth, then stir in the crushed tomatoes, bay leaf, and House Seasoning to taste. Drain the beans and discard the liquid. Add the beans to the soup, stir, and bring to a boil. Reduce the heat, cover, and simmer for 2 hours, or until the beans are as tender as you like. Thin the soup with the chicken broth. Remove and discard the bay leaf. Ladle the soup into bowls and sprinkle with bacon. 🍀 🍀 🍀 **The Lady & Sons**

Taco Soup

SERVES 12–16

2 pounds ground beef
2 cups chopped onions
Two 15½-ounce cans pink kidney
  beans
Two 15½-ounce cans pinto beans
One 15¼-ounce can niblet corn,
  drained
One 14½-ounce can Del Monte
  Mexican tomatoes
One 14½-ounce can diced
  tomatoes
One 14½-ounce can Del Monte
  tomatoes with chilies
Two 4½-ounce cans diced green
  chilies

1 small can black olives, drained
  and sliced (optional)
½ cup green olives, sliced (optional)
One 1¼-ounce package taco
  seasoning mix
One 1-ounce package Hidden
  Valley Original Ranch salad
  dressing mix
Corn chips
Sour cream
Grated cheese
Chopped onions

Brown the ground beef and onions in a large skillet; drain the excess fat, then transfer the browned beef and onions to a large crockpot or a stockpot. Add the beans, corn, tomatoes, chilies, olives, and seasonings, and cook on low setting all day (6 to 8 hours) if using a crockpot, or simmer over low heat for about 1 hour in a stockpot on the stove. To serve, place a few corn chips in each bowl and ladle soup over them. Top with sour cream, cheese, and onions.

Homemade Dried Onion Soup Mix

MAKES THE EQUIVALENT OF ONE ⅕-OUNCE PACKAGE
OF DRIED ONION SOUP MIX

½ teaspoon onion powder
½ teaspoon salt
¼ teaspoon sugar

¼ teaspoon Kitchen Bouquet
½ cup dehydrated onion

Combine the onion powder, salt, and sugar in a small bowl. Add the Kitchen Bouquet and stir until the mixture is uniformly brown. Add the onion and mix thoroughly until the color is again even (this step takes several minutes).

Hawaiian Chicken Salad

SERVES 8–10

This is wonderful served on croissants or on a bed of lettuce. It also makes a nice appetizer served in miniature phyllo shells.

4 cups cubed cooked chicken breast
  (4 large breasts)
2 cups diced celery
1 cup mayonnaise
1 cup sliced almonds
Two 11-ounce cans mandarin
  oranges, drained

One 20-ounce can pineapple
  tidbits, drained
1 pound seedless green grapes, cut
  in half

In a large bowl, combine the chicken, celery, mayonnaise, and almonds, and mix well. Gently fold in the oranges, pineapple, and grapes.

Nancy's Cole Slaw

SERVES 8 OR MORE

1 medium onion, chopped
1 cup sugar
1 cup vegetable oil
½ cup cider vinegar
⅓ cup mayonnaise

1 teaspoon salt
½ teaspoon celery seed
1 medium green cabbage, cored
  and shredded

In a medium bowl, combine the onion and sugar and let stand for 30 minutes. In a separate bowl, combine the oil, vinegar, mayonnaise, salt, and celery seed and add to the onion mixture. Pour the mixture into a jar with a tight lid. Shake the jar to blend the dressing. Put the cabbage in a large serving bowl and add the onions, pour on the dressing, and toss well. Do not overdress.

Pecan Cranberry Salad

SERVES 12

One 15-ounce can crushed
    pineapple, drained, 1 cup of
    juice reserved
1 cup water
One 3-ounce package orange
    gelatin dessert mix
One 3-ounce package cherry
    gelatin dessert mix

One 16-ounce can whole-berry
    cranberry sauce
One 6-ounce can frozen orange
    juice concentrate
1 cup chopped pecans or walnuts
½ cup chopped celery (optional)

Combine the pineapple juice (from the can) and the water in a small saucepan; bring to a boil and remove from the heat. Pour the juice mixture into a large bowl and add the gelatin dessert mixes; stir until dissolved. Add the drained pineapple, cranberry sauce, orange juice concentrate, nuts, and celery, and mix well. Spray a 6-cup mold with nonstick cooking spray. Pour the gelatin mixture into the mold and refrigerate until firm.

Golda's Frozen Waldorf Salad

SERVES 8

½ cup sugar
½ cup pineapple juice
¼ cup fresh lemon juice
⅛ teaspoon salt
½ cup diced celery
½ cup miniature marshmallows
½ cup red seedless grapes, cut in half

½ cup crushed pineapple, drained
2 medium apples, diced, skins left
    on
½ cup broken walnuts or pecans
1⅓ cups heavy cream
8 fresh or maraschino cherries
Fresh mint leaves

In a saucepan, combine the sugar, pineapple juice, lemon juice, and salt. Cook over medium heat, stirring constantly, until thick. Let cool, then stir in the celery, marshmallows, grapes, pineapple, apples and nuts. Whip the cream and fold it into the fruit mixture. Spoon into an 8 × 8-inch pan and freeze.

Remove the salad from the freezer 5 minutes before serving and cut into squares. Garnish each serving with a fresh or maraschino cherry and fresh mint leaves.

Feta Cheese and Tomato Salad

SERVES 6–8

6 medium tomatoes (about 2½ pounds), cut into wedges
1½ cups crumbled feta cheese
¼–½ cup chopped green onions
3 tablespoons olive oil

2 cloves garlic, minced
1 teaspoon dried oregano or 1 tablespoon fresh
The Lady's House Seasoning
Boston lettuce leaves

In a large bowl, combine the tomatoes, cheese, onions, oil, garlic, and oregano. Toss gently and refrigerate at least 2 hours. At serving time, add House Seasoning to taste. Spoon the salad onto a bed of lettuce leaves. Serve with a good crusty bread.　❦ ❦ ❦　**The Lady & Sons**

Chinese Salad

SERVES 12

2 heads Napa or Bok Choy cabbage
6 green onions
Two 3-ounce packages ramen noodles with seasoning packets
One 6-ounce package slivered almonds

2 tablespoons sesame seeds
1 cup vegetable oil
½ cup sugar
6 tablespoons white vinegar
½ teaspoon salt

Tear the cabbage into bite-size pieces and slice the onions. Combine them in a large salad bowl. Crumble the noodles into a broiler pan, add the almonds and sesame seeds, and broil for 2 minutes, being careful not to scorch the sesame seeds. In a jar with a tight lid, combine the oil, sugar, vinegar, and salt with the contents of the seasoning packets. Cover the jar and shake to blend the dressing. Just before serving, pour the dressing over the salad and toss to combine.

Gingersnap Pear Salad

SERVES 8

10 gingersnaps
One 3-ounce package cream cheese,
   at room temperature

1 tablespoon mayonnaise
8 canned pear halves, drained
Chilled crisp lettuce

Crush the gingersnaps to very fine crumbs. The easy way to do this is to put them in a plastic bag and crush them with a rolling pin. Put the cookie crumbs in a bowl, add the cream cheese and mayonnaise, and mix well. Place the pear halves on a bed of lettuce and fill the hollows with the cream cheese mixture.

Pickled Beets and Eggs

SERVES 6

One 15-ounce can whole beets,
   drained, juice reserved
¾ cup sugar
½ cup malt vinegar

½ teaspoon whole cloves
1 teaspoon salt
6 hard-boiled eggs, peeled and
   rinsed

Combine the reserved beet juice, sugar, vinegar, cloves, and salt in a saucepan and heat until the sugar has dissolved. Place the eggs in a large bowl, then add the beets. Pour in the juice, cover, and refrigerate overnight.

Spinach, Strawberry, and Hearts of Palm Salad

SERVES 12

⅓ cup cider vinegar
¾ cup sugar
2 tablespoons fresh lemon juice
1 teaspoon salt
1 cup vegetable oil
½ small red onion, grated
1½ tablespoons poppy seeds
1 teaspoon dry mustard

½ teaspoon paprika
1½ pounds fresh spinach, washed
    and torn into pieces
1 can hearts of palm, drained and
    chopped
2 cups strawberries, stemmed and
    sliced
1 cup chopped walnuts

For the dressing, combine the vinegar, sugar, lemon juice, and salt in a saucepan and heat until the sugar dissolves, stirring frequently. Cool to room temperature. Whisk in the oil, onion, poppy seeds, dry mustard, and paprika, and set aside. Combine the spinach, hearts of palm, strawberries, and walnuts in a salad bowl. Add a little of the dressing at serving time and toss gently. Serve the remaining dressing alongside, so guests may help themselves.

Blueberry Salad

SERVES 8–10

Two 3-ounce packages grape
    gelatin dessert mix
2 cups boiling water
One 21-ounce can blueberry pie
    filling
One 20-ounce can crushed
    pineapple

One 8-ounce package cream cheese,
    at room temperature
1 cup sour cream
1 cup pecan halves
1 teaspoon vanilla extract

In a large bowl, mix the gelatin dessert mix into the boiling water. When the powder has dissolved, stir in the blueberry pie filling and the pineapple with its juice. Pour into a 13 × 9-inch shallow baking dish.

Refrigerate for at least 4 hours, or overnight. Stir together the cream cheese, sour cream, pecans, and vanilla. Spread this mixture over the jelled salad. Chill for an additional hour.

Marinated Asparagus Salad

SERVES 10–12

2 bunches asparagus, trimmed and
  cooked, or three 15-ounce cans
  whole green asparagus spears
1 teaspoon dried tarragon leaves
Black pepper

1 teaspoon garlic salt
Two 0.7-ounce packages Italian
  salad dressing mix, prepared
  according to package directions
½ cup tarragon vinegar

Drain the asparagus and layer it in a shallow glass dish. Sprinkle each layer with some crumbled tarragon, pepper to taste, and garlic salt. Pour the salad dressing and vinegar over the asparagus, cover, and let stand overnight at room temperature. To serve, refrigerate until well chilled. Serve the asparagus on lettuce leaves, topped with a dollop of mayonnaise flavored with a little of the dressing.

Fettuccine Chicken Salad

SERVES 8

4 large boneless skinless chicken
  breast halves
2 teaspoons The Lady's House
  Seasoning
2 tablespoons chopped fresh
  thyme
3 tablespoons olive oil

Two 9-ounce packages fresh
  fettuccine
2 cups mayonnaise
½ cup chopped green onion tops
¼ cup chopped fresh parsley
¼ cup chopped fresh basil
1 teaspoon The Lady's Seasoned Salt

Slice the chicken breasts lengthwise into 1-inch wide strips. Sprinkle with 1 teaspoon of the House Seasoning and thyme, place on a baking sheet, and drizzle with olive oil. Bake at 350 degrees for 15 to 20 minutes or until cooked through but still juicy; do not overcook. While the chicken is cooking, cook the pasta according to package directions. Drain the pasta, rinse in cold water, and drain again. Pat excess moisture off the pasta with a paper towel if necessary.

Remove the chicken from the pan and set aside. Pour the juices from the pan into a bowl. Add the mayonnaise, green onions, parsley, basil, the remaining teaspoon of House Seasoning, and the Seasoned Salt. Pour the dressing over the pasta and toss gently. Place the chicken strips on top of the pasta. Garnish with tomato wedges and additional sliced green onion tops. You may make this dish the day before serving. ❦ ❦ ❦ *The Lady & Sons*

Colo Cucumber Salad

SERVES 4

2 cucumbers	*½ cup mayonnaise*
1 teaspoon salt	*¼ cup sour cream*
1 teaspoon vinegar	*1 tablespoon fresh dill*

Peel and slice the cucumbers and put them in a glass bowl. Sprinkle them with salt and vinegar. Cover and let stand for ½ hour. Pour off the excess liquid. Add the mayonnaise, sour cream, and dill, and mix well. Cover and refrigerate until serving time. ❦ ❦ ❦ *The Lady & Sons*

Thanksgiving Apple Salad

SERVES 8

¾ cup sugar	*¼ cup (½ stick) butter*
⅓ cup all-purpose flour	*3–4 large red apples, diced*
1 cup heavy cream	*1 cup chopped nuts*
One 20-ounce can crushed pineapple, drained	*½ cup halved maraschino cherries*

Stir together the sugar and flour. Whisk in the cream. Pour the cream mixture into a heavy nonaluminum saucepan. Continue mixing, add the pineapple, and cook over medium heat, whisking constantly, until the mixture thickens. Add the butter; remove the pan from the heat and let the mixture cool. When cooled, add the apples, nuts, and cherries, and mix well. Refrigerate until ready to serve.

❦ ❦ ❦   **The Lady & Sons**

Fruit Salad with Honey Dressing

SERVES 6

⅓ cup honey
¼ cup orange juice
¼ cup vegetable oil
½ teaspoon fresh lemon juice, plus the juice of 1 lemon
1½ teaspoons poppy seeds
¼ teaspoon salt
¼ teaspoon prepared mustard

1 apple, cored and diced
1 banana, sliced
1 avocado, peeled and sliced
One 11-ounce can mandarin oranges, drained
¼ cup raisins
¼ cup chopped walnuts or pecans

For the dressing, combine the honey, orange juice, oil, ½ teaspoon lemon juice, poppy seeds, salt, and mustard in a jar with a tight lid; cover and shake well. Toss the apple, banana, and avocado with juice from 1 lemon to prevent the fruit from turning brown. Combine the fruit, raisins, and nuts in a glass bowl. Add the dressing and stir gently. Serve on red leaf lettuce.

My Mother's Congealed Salad

SERVES 12–15

1½ cups water
One 3-ounce package lemon gelatin dessert mix
One 3-ounce package lime gelatin dessert mix

One 20-ounce can crushed pineapple, drained
½ cup orange juice
½ cup evaporated milk
1 tablespoon fresh lemon juice

1 cup mayonnaise
½ cup cottage cheese
½ cup chopped walnuts

½ cup cherries, cut in half
Prepared horseradish
Pinch of salt

Bring the water to a boil and stir in the gelatin mixes until dissolved. Let cool slightly, then add the pineapple, orange juice, evaporated milk, and lemon juice. Refrigerate until slightly thickened. Mix together the mayonnaise, cottage cheese, nuts, cherries, horseradish to taste, and salt. Stir this mixture into the gelatin. Pour into a lightly greased 13 × 9 × 2-inch pan and refrigerate until firm.

Copper Pennies

SERVES 12–15

1 cup sugar
¾ cup white vinegar
½ cup vegetable oil
1 teaspoon dry mustard
1 teaspoon Worcestershire sauce
1 teaspoon salt
¾ teaspoon coarsely ground black
  pepper

One 10¾-ounce can tomato soup
2 pounds carrots, peeled, cooked,
  and sliced
1 medium onion, sliced into rings
1 green bell pepper, coarsely
  chopped

Combine the sugar, vinegar, oil, mustard, Worcestershire sauce, salt, and pepper in a saucepan over medium heat and bring to a boil. Remove from the heat and add the soup. Mix the carrots, onion, and bell pepper together in a large glass dish; pour the sauce over the vegetables, stir gently to combine, and refrigerate overnight. This salad will keep for up to 6 weeks in the refrigerator. ❧ ❧ ❧ **The Lady & Sons**

Strawberry Mold

SERVES 12

Two 3-ounce packages strawberry
   gelatin dessert mix
1 cup boiling water
Two 10-ounce packages frozen
   strawberries

3 medium bananas, mashed
1 cup crushed canned pineapple,
   drained
1 cup chopped pecans
1 cup sour cream

Add the gelatin dessert mix to the boiling water and stir until dissolved. Add the strawberries, bananas, pineapple, and nuts. Pour half of the mixture into a 13 × 9-inch casserole; refrigerate until set. Cover with a layer of sour cream, then top with the remaining gelatin mixture. Refrigerate until firm; cut into squares to serve.

Fruit Bowl

SERVES 12–15

3 tablespoons orange Tang
   Breakfast Drink mix
One 15½-ounce can pineapple
   chunks, drained, juice reserved
One 3.4-ounce box instant lemon
   pudding mix
One 16-ounce can chunky mixed
   fruit, drained

One 11-ounce can mandarin
   oranges, drained
One 6-ounce jar maraschino
   cherries
3 large bananas

Stir the Tang into the pineapple juice. Add the lemon pudding mix and stir well. Combine the pineapple, mixed fruit, oranges, and cherries, then mix the fruit and pudding mixtures together; toss well. Refrigerate until ready to serve. Just before serving, slice and add the bananas.   ❦ ❦ ❦ **The Lady & Sons**

Warm Apple and Goat Cheese Salad

SERVES 4

2 tablespoons raspberry vinegar or
   red wine vinegar
½ teaspoon Dijon mustard
1 small clove garlic, minced
½ teaspoon salt
½ teaspoon pepper
⅓ cup olive oil
1 tablespoon chopped fresh parsley
3 Belgian endives, cored and
   separated into leaves

1 bunch watercress or spinach,
   washed
1 Granny Smith apple, sliced
4 ounces mild goat cheese, from a
   small log
¼ cup chopped walnuts

In a glass jar with a tight lid, combine the vinegar, mustard, garlic, salt, and pepper and shake to blend. Add the oil and parsley and shake again.

    Arrange the endive leaves like spokes on 4 plates; arrange the watercress or spinach in the center. Preheat the broiler. Arrange the apple slices, slightly overlapping, in 4 fans in a broiler pan. Cut the cheese into 4 slices and top each fan of apples with a slice of cheese. Broil until golden, about 5 minutes. With a spatula, carefully place the apple slices and cheese on top of the endive. Drizzle dressing over the salads and sprinkle with walnuts. Serve at once.

Cherry Tomato
and Mushroom Salad

SERVES 8–10

1 pound cherry tomatoes
1 pound fresh mushrooms
¼ cup vegetable oil
½ cup cider vinegar

One 0.7-ounce package Italian
   salad dressing mix
Coarsely ground black pepper

Cut the cherry tomatoes in half. Halve any particularly large mushrooms. In a glass jar with a tight lid, combine the oil, vinegar, salad dressing mix, and pepper to taste. Combine the tomatoes and mushrooms in a salad bowl; pour on the dressing, and toss.

❦ ❦ ❦   *The Lady & Sons*

Strawberry Pretzel Salad

SERVES 8–10

2 cups crushed pretzels
¾ cup (1½ sticks) melted butter
3 tablespoons, plus ¾ cup sugar
One 8-ounce package cream cheese
One 8-ounce carton Cool Whip
Two 3-ounce packages strawberry
  gelatin dessert mix

2 cups boiling water
Two 10-ounce packages frozen
  strawberries
1 small can crushed pineapple

Preheat the oven to 400 degrees. For the crust, mix the pretzels, butter, and 3 tablespoons sugar. Press this mixture into a 9 × 13-inch pan. Bake for 7 minutes and set aside to cool. Beat together the cream cheese and ¾ cup sugar. Fold in the Cool Whip and spread over the cooled crust. Refrigerate until well chilled. Dissolve the gelatin dessert mix in the boiling water; cool slightly. Add the strawberries and pineapple, and pour over the cream-cheese mixture. Refrigerate until serving time.

Marinated Shrimp and Artichoke Hearts

SERVES 10–12

1 cup vegetable oil
½ cup red wine vinegar
⅓ cup dry white wine

1 tablespoon snipped fresh parsley
  or 1 teaspoon dry
1 teaspoon sugar

½ teaspoon salt

½ teaspoon paprika

¼ teaspoon whole black peppercorns

1 clove garlic, minced

2 pounds medium shrimp, cooked
   and peeled

Two 14-ounce cans artichoke
   hearts, drained and halved

One 8-ounce can sliced water
   chestnuts, drained

1 small red onion, thinly sliced
   into rings

Cherry tomatoes, for garnish

In a jar with a tight lid, combine the oil, vinegar, wine, parsley, sugar, salt, paprika, peppercorns, and garlic. Cover and shake well. In a 4-quart food-storage container, combine the shrimp, artichoke hearts, water chestnuts, and onion. Pour on the marinade, cover the container tightly, and shake it to coat the shrimp and vegetables with marinade. Refrigerate overnight, stirring occasionally. Serve this as a first course, garnished with cherry tomatoes.

Main Courses

FISH AND SHELLFISH

Shrimp and Rice Croquettes with Aioli

Shrimp and Grits with Marinara Sauce

Shrimp Gravy

Battered Fried Shrimp

Grilled Red Pepper Scallops

Beaufort Shrimp Pie

Stewed Salmon

The Lady's Bouillabaisse

Trey's Baked Grouper Parmigiano

Grouper Fromage

Wild Rice and Oyster Casserole

Can't-Miss Red Snapper

Easy Shrimp Bake

The Best Crab Casserole

Ginger Shrimp

Fiery Cajun Shrimp

Barbara's Mussels

Baked Shrimp-Crab Salad

Tuna Burgers

Nootsie's Chesapeake Bay Crab Cakes

MEAT

Brandied Prime Rib

Ron's Grilled Peanut Butter Ham

Bubba's Country-Fried Venison Steak

Prince Charles' Calf's Liver

Fried Veal

Perfect Eye-of-Round Roast

Spiced Beef with Dumplin's

Sunday Morning Casserole

Baked Pasta Florentine

Stuffed Red Peppers

The Lady & Sons Smoked Boston Butt Roast

Fried Spare Ribs

Duxelles-Stuffed Tenderloin

The Lady & Sons Pot Roast

Roast Pork with Plum Sauce

Baked Spaghetti

Pepper Steak

Venison Wellington with Oyster Pâté

Wayne's Beef Macaroni and Cheese

The Lady's Pork Stew

St. Paddy's Day Corned Beef and Cabbage

Sausage with Ravishing Rice

Dixieland Pork Chops

Barbecued Short Ribs

Texas-Style Chili

Ron's Tybee Island Sausage Pie

Steak Diane

Barbecue Meat Loaf

Perfect Char-Grilled Filet Mignon

POULTRY

Hot Savannah Chicken Salad Casserole

Mexican Chicken

Hurry-Up Chicken Pot Pie

Quail with Marsala Sauce

Chicken with Drop Dumplin's

Basil Grilled Chicken

Chicken Bog

Chicken Casserole

Fricasé de Pollo

Chicken Boudine

Chicken Florentine

Pat's Almond Chicken Casserole

Saucy Chicken and Asparagus Bake

Szechuan Chicken with Angelhair Pasta

Savannah Gumbo

Chicken and Wild Rice Casserole

Shrimp and Rice Croquettes with Aioli

SERVES 4

AIOLI
2 egg yolks
1 tablespoon prepared mustard
5 cloves garlic
¾ cup olive oil
1 tablespoon fresh lemon juice
½ teaspoon salt
½ teaspoon pepper

CROQUETTES
½ cup rice
1 tablespoon butter
2 cups minced cooked shrimp
½ cup finely chopped green onions
2 tablespoons fresh lemon juice
The Lady's House Seasoning
3 tablespoons all-purpose flour
2 eggs, lightly beaten
Breadcrumbs or cracker crumbs
1½ cups vegetable oil

For the aioli, combine the egg yolks, mustard, and garlic in the bowl of a food processor. Start the machine and add ½ cup of the oil in a fine stream. Add the lemon juice, salt, and pepper, then add the remaining oil, and process until thick and smooth. Refrigerate until needed.

For the croquettes, cook the rice in 1 cup boiling salted water for 20 minutes or until done. Add the butter while the rice is still hot. Add the shrimp, onions, lemon juice, and House Seasoning to taste. Stir in the flour and eggs. Refrigerate this mixture for 2 hours.

Shape the rice mixture into patties and coat with bread- or cracker crumbs. Heat the oil in a 10-inch cast-iron skillet. Oil should be hot but not smoking. Fry the croquettes over medium-high heat until nice and golden brown on both sides. Drain on paper towels. Serve with aioli.

Shrimp and Grits with Marinara Sauce

SERVES 4–6

2 medium Vidalia onions, coarsely
  chopped
1 large green bell pepper, seeded
  and coarsely chopped
2 tablespoons vegetable oil
1 pound large shrimp, peeled and
  deveined
Cayenne pepper
Chili powder

6 servings creamy white grits,
  cooked in milk or chicken broth
2–3 cups Marinara Sauce
  (recipe follows, or use store-
  bought)
¼ cup freshly grated Parmesan
¼ cup chopped fresh parsley or basil

Sauté the onions and bell pepper in oil until crisp-tender. Add the shrimp and sauté until pink, 2 to 3 minutes. Season with cayenne pepper and chili powder to taste. Add the cooked grits. Spoon grits into individual serving bowls, and ladle ½ cup Marinara Sauce over each serving. Sprinkle with the Parmesan and parsley or basil. Re-season, if necessary, with cayenne pepper and chili powder. Serve with crusty garlic bread.

MARINARA SAUCE

MAKES ABOUT 3 QUARTS

4 tablespoons olive oil
1 medium onion, diced
1 green bell pepper, diced
2 tablespoons minced garlic (4 or
  5 cloves)
1 tablespoon chopped fresh basil
1 tablespoon chopped fresh thyme

1 tablespoon chopped fresh oregano
½ cup red wine
Two 28-ounce cans diced tomatoes
Two 29-ounce cans tomato sauce
2 tablespoons sugar
2 teaspoons The Lady's House
  Seasoning

Heat the oil in a large, heavy pot over medium heat, then sauté the onions, bell pepper, and garlic until the onion is translucent (be careful not to burn the garlic). Stir often to keep the vegetables from sticking. Add the herbs and continue to stir for 1 minute. Add the wine (pour yourself a glass as well and enjoy) and cook, stirring for 1 minute longer. Add the diced tomatoes and stir for 2 minutes, then add the tomato sauce, sugar, and House Seasoning. Reduce the heat and simmer, stirring occasionally, for at least 2 hours. The longer it cooks, the thicker it gets. Freeze any extra.

Shrimp Gravy

SERVES 4

2 strips bacon
¼ cup chopped onion
2 cups uncooked shrimp, peeled and deveined (small ones preferred)

2 tablespoons all-purpose flour
¼ cup ketchup
1 teaspoon Worcestershire sauce
1½–2 cups water
The Lady's House Seasoning

Fry the bacon in a heavy skillet and remove from the pan; set aside. Sauté the onion in the bacon grease until soft. Add the shrimp and stir for a minute or two. Stir in the flour until the shrimp are coated. Add the ketchup and Worcestershire sauce, then slowly stir in 1½ to 2 cups of water—enough to make a good gravy. Add House Seasoning to taste. Serve with grits for breakfast or brunch.

Battered Fried Shrimp

SERVES 4–6

1 cup all-purpose flour
½ teaspoon sugar
½ teaspoon salt
1 cup ice water
1 egg

2 tablespoons melted fat or vegetable oil
2 pounds uncooked shrimp, peeled and deveined, tails left on
Vegetable oil for deep frying

In a large bowl stir together the flour, sugar, and salt. Beat in the ice water, egg, and 2 tablespoons fat or oil. Dry the shrimp thoroughly. Heat the oil for deep frying in a large, heavy pot until it registers 375 degrees. Holding the shrimp by the tails, dip them in batter. Carefully place them in the pot and fry until golden brown. Do *not* overcook; just a few minutes does the trick. Drain on paper towels and serve immediately.

Grilled Red Pepper Scallops

SERVES 6

1½ pounds large sea scallops
2 tablespoons olive oil
Zest of one lemon

Freshly ground black pepper
4 large red bell peppers

In a bowl, combine the scallops, olive oil, lemon zest, and black pepper to taste. Preheat the broiler or prepare coals for outdoor grilling. Cut the bell peppers in half lengthwise and remove the stems, seeds, and ribs. If cooking in a broiler, place the peppers cut-side down on a baking sheet.

Broil or grill the peppers until blackened, 6 to 10 minutes. Transfer to a paper bag, close the top and let steam for 10 minutes. Remove the charred skins and cut the peppers lengthwise into ¾-inch strips. Wrap a pepper strip around each scallop to cover completely, overlapping the pepper ends. Secure the strips by running a 10-inch metal skewer through the scallop and pepper. Use 6 skewers; add scallops to each skewer until filled. Grill skewers over a medium-hot fire, turning once, until scallops are almost firm to the touch, 1 to 2 minutes on each side. Alternatively, cook under the broiler for about 3 minutes per side. Serve immediately.

Beaufort Shrimp Pie

SERVES 6–8

In the Carolina Sea Islands, a "pie" does not necessarily have a crust. This shrimp casserole is a superb luncheon dish and is one of these pies.

½ cup chopped onion
¼ cup chopped green bell pepper
2 tablespoons butter
3 cups cooked and peeled shrimp
2 cups soft breadcrumbs

2 cups milk
2 eggs
Salt and pepper
3 strips bacon

Sauté the onion and bell pepper in butter until soft. In a casserole, make layers of the shrimp, breadcrumbs, and the onions and peppers. Beat together the milk, eggs, and salt and pepper to taste, and pour over the shrimp. Cut each strip of bacon into 4 pieces. Lay bacon on top of the casserole and bake at 325 degrees until the filling is set and the bacon is brown. ❦ ❦ ❦ **The Lady & Sons**

Stewed Salmon

SERVES 3–4

We sometimes serve this on our buffet, if the staff doesn't eat it all first!

1 medium onion, diced
4 tablespoons butter
One 14¾-ounce can salmon
1½ cups water

1 teaspoon The Lady's House
    Seasoning
½ teaspoon Accent (optional)

In a large skillet, sauté the onion in butter until tender. Turn the salmon out of the can, saving the liquid. Pick the salmon free of bones (some folks like the bones, and I am one of them). Add the salmon and its liquid, along with the water, to the skillet. Add the House Seasoning and Accent, if using, and simmer for 10 minutes. Serve hot over grits or rice. ❦ ❦ ❦ **The Lady & Sons**

The Lady's Bouillabaisse

SERVES 8

This dish is a specialty of the South of France, but living or visiting on the coast of Georgia you are quite likely to see it offered on menus. I hope you enjoy The Lady & Sons' version of this wonderful French dish. Feel free to add any of your favorite shellfish to the pot.

2 pounds mussels

2 cups water

2 pounds firm fresh fish fillets such
    as grouper or striped bass (ask
    your local fishmonger for
    additional suggestions)

¾ cup olive oil

1½ tablespoons finely chopped garlic

1½ cups chopped onions

5 Roma tomatoes, peeled and
    sliced, or 2 cups canned Italian
    tomatoes

2 teaspoons fennel seed

¼ teaspoon saffron

1 tablespoon, plus ½ teaspoon
    kosher salt

1½ teaspoons freshly ground pepper

5 cups boiling water

One 8-ounce bottle clam juice

4 whole crabs, cut in half

1 pound unpeeled shrimp

1 loaf French bread

Butter

Wash and scrub the mussels in cold water. Bring 2 cups of water to a boil in a large, heavy pot. Add the mussels and cover the pot. Steam for 6 to 8 minutes, or until the mussels open. Discard any mussels that didn't open. Remove from the heat and set aside. Cut the fish into 1-inch thick slices. Heat the oil in a large pot. Add the garlic, onions, tomatoes, fennel, saffron, salt, and pepper. Add the boiling water and clam juice. Bring to a rolling boil, add the crabs and fish, and continue to boil for 6 to 8 minutes. Add the mussels and their broth to the pot along with the shrimp, and boil for an additional 5 minutes.

Slice the French bread, butter it, and toast lightly. Serve the bouillabaisse in large individual bowls lined with toasted French bread; pile in the seafood and ladle the broth over it. Top each bowl with 1 tablespoon of butter. Pass the remaining bread at the table. If you like a spicier soup you may add a couple of whole hot peppers to the pot at the start of cooking.   ❦ ❦ ❦ **The Lady & Sons**

Trey's Baked Grouper Parmigiano

SERVES 2

We have many good local seafood suppliers here on the coast, but one that has consistently been there to serve me with good, fresh seafood, day in and day out, is Mathews Seafood. This business was started years ago by Louis Mathews. Today, his three sons, Chris, Trey, and John, carry on in their father's footsteps. I can always count on these young men to guide us in selecting the best they have to offer. Thanks, guys!

Butter	*3 teaspoons fresh lemon juice*
Two 8-ounce grouper fillets	*1 tablespoon minced fresh dill*
½ cup mayonnaise	*Black pepper*
¼ cup freshly grated Parmesan	*½ teaspoon paprika*

Preheat the oven to 350 degrees. Butter a baking dish. Place the grouper fillets in the dish. In a small bowl, whisk together the mayonnaise, Parmesan, lemon juice, dill, and pepper to taste, and spread this over the fish. Sprinkle with paprika and bake for 10 minutes, or until just cooked through.

Grouper Fromage

SERVES 4

Rance, the young man who has the large task of managing our kitchen, still finds time to prepare this all-time favorite dish for our dinner guests. We love you, Rance!

1 cup mayonnaise	*1 teaspoon The Lady's House*
2 cups shredded Monterey Jack	* Seasoning*
* cheese*	*4 grouper fillets, about 8 ounces*
½ cup sautéed chopped onion	* each*
1 teaspoon Texas Pete Hot Sauce	*1 lemon*
1 teaspoon ground red pepper	

Mix together the mayonnaise, cheese, onion, hot sauce, red pepper, and ½ teaspoon House Seasoning; set aside.

Preheat the oven to 350 degrees. Grease a 13 × 9 × 2-inch baking dish. Add just enough water to come to a depth of ¼ inch. Sprinkle the fish with the remaining ½ teaspoon of House Seasoning. Place the fish in the baking dish and squeeze the juice of the lemon over it. Bake for 10 to 20 minutes; the time will depend on the thickness of your fish. When the fish is almost done, remove the dish from the oven and cover each fillet with ½ cup of the cheese mixture. Return to the oven and continue to bake for 8 to 10 minutes longer.   ❦ ❦ ❦   **The Lady & Sons**

Wild Rice and Oyster Casserole

SERVES 10–12

One 10¾-ounce can beef broth	Salt and pepper
2½ cups water	One 10¾-ounce can cream of
2 cups raw Mahatma Long Grain	mushroom soup
and Wild Rice with Seasoning	1 cup half-and-half
¾ cup (1½ sticks) butter	1½ teaspoons onion powder
2 quarts oysters, very well drained	½ teaspoon garlic salt
4 dashes Texas Pete Hot Sauce	½ cup finely minced fresh parsley

Preheat the oven to 350 degrees. In a saucepan, bring the beef broth and water to a boil. Add the rice, bring to a boil again, reduce heat, and simmer covered for 25 minutes. Drain any liquid remaining. Add ½ cup of the butter and stir; fluff with a fork.

Sauté the drained oysters in ¼ cup of the butter over medium-high heat until the edges curl, approximately 3 to 5 minutes. Remove the oysters with a slotted spoon; set aside. Place half of the rice in a greased 13 × 9 × 2-inch baking dish. Cover it with oysters and sprinkle with hot sauce and salt and pepper to taste. Top with the remaining rice.

In a saucepan, heat the mushroom soup over medium heat. Add the half-and-half, onion powder, and garlic salt. Pour over the oyster mixture. Bake for 35 to 40 minutes, until golden brown and bubbling. Garnish with parsley.

Can't-Miss Red Snapper

SERVES 4

Four 8-ounce red snapper fillets,
    ½ inch thick
1 teaspoon salt
½ teaspoon pepper
1 tablespoon Worcestershire sauce

1 cup chopped onions
1 chopped green bell pepper
½ cup (1 stick) butter
1 cup freshly grated Parmesan

Season the fish with the salt, pepper, and Worcestershire sauce. Spread the onions and pepper in a 13 × 9 × 2-inch metal baking pan and place the fish on top. Dot the fish with butter. Bake in a 350-degree oven for 8 minutes, then baste with the pan juices. Cook for 8 minutes longer, basting again. Bake for a final 8 minutes, continuing to baste with the juices. Cover the fish with Parmesan and place under the broiler until the cheese browns. To serve, spoon the vegetables over the fish.

Easy Shrimp Bake

SERVES 6

1 cup sliced fresh mushrooms
4 green onions, chopped
2 tablespoons butter
2 cups cooked and peeled shrimp
6–8 slices of day-old bread,
    trimmed, buttered, and cubed
½ pound sharp cheese, grated

3 eggs
½ teaspoon salt
½ teaspoon dry mustard
Pinch of pepper
Pinch of paprika
1½ cups milk

In a skillet, sauté the mushrooms and onions in butter. Grease a 2-quart casserole. Put the shrimp, the mushrooms, the onions, half of the bread cubes, and half of the cheese in the casserole, and stir gently. Top with rest of the cheese and bread cubes. Lightly beat the eggs with the salt, mustard, pepper, and paprika. Stir in the milk and pour into the casserole. If making this dish the day before serving, cover and refrigerate. Bake at 325 degrees for 40 to 50 minutes, or until set and golden brown. ❦ ❦ ❦ **The Lady & Sons**

The Best Crab Casserole

SERVES 4–6

*One 6½-ounce can crabmeat,
    drained*
1 cup mayonnaise
1 cup soft breadcrumbs
¾ cup half-and-half
6 hard-boiled eggs, finely chopped
½ cup chopped onion

¼ cup sliced stuffed green olives
2 tablespoons chopped fresh parsley
¾ teaspoon salt
Pinch of pepper
½ cup buttered soft breadcrumbs
Olive slices, for garnish

In a large bowl, break up the crabmeat in chunks. Add the mayonnaise, soft breadcrumbs, half-and-half, eggs, onion, olives, parsley, salt, and pepper, and fold together. Divide the mixture among greased individual bakers or spoon it into a 1-quart casserole dish. Top with the buttered crumbs and bake at 350 degrees for 20 to 25 minutes. Garnish with olive slices. ❦ ❦ ❦ **The Lady & Sons**

Ginger Shrimp

SERVES 4

1 tablespoon vegetable oil
*1½ pounds shrimp, peeled and
    deveined*
2 tablespoons grated fresh ginger

1 cup chopped green onions (about 5)
1½ cups chicken broth
2 tablespoons cold water
1 tablespoon cornstarch

Heat 1½ teaspoons of oil in a large nonstick skillet and sauté the shrimp until they turn a light pink, about 4 minutes. Remove the shrimp and set aside. Heat the remaining oil over medium-low heat, add the ginger and onions, and sauté until onions are tender. Add the chicken broth and bring to a boil. Mix together the water and cornstarch and stir the mixture into the skillet; the sauce will thicken in about 1 minute. Return the shrimp to the skillet and bring the sauce to a boil. Serve over your favorite rice.

Fiery Cajun Shrimp

SERVES 8

2 cups (4 sticks) melted butter
½ cup Worcestershire sauce
¼ cup fresh lemon juice
¼ cup ground pepper
2 teaspoons Texas Pete Hot Sauce

4 cloves garlic, minced
2 teaspoons salt
5 pounds unpeeled medium
    shrimp
2 lemons, thinly sliced

Stir together the butter, Worcestershire sauce, lemon juice, pepper, hot sauce, garlic, and salt. Pour half this mixture into a large heatproof dish. Layer half the shrimp and half the lemon slices in the dish; then form a second layer with the remaining shrimp and lemon slices, and pour remaining sauce into the dish. Bake, uncovered, at 400 degrees for 20 minutes, or until the shrimp are pink, stirring twice. Pour off the sauce into individual serving dishes. Serve the shrimp with plenty of French bread for dipping in the spicy butter sauce.

Barbara's Mussels

SERVES 4

This can be done with mussels and clams mixed, and you can also add shrimp at the end if you like variety.

2 pounds mussels*
2 cups wine (Chardonnay or
  Cabernet)
One 14½-ounce can Italian-style
  chopped tomatoes
½ cup (1 stick) butter, cut into
  quarters

½ cup fresh or 1 cup minced garlic
  from a jar**
1-ounce bunch fresh basil, chopped
2 shallots, chopped

Rinse and scrub the mussels in cold water. Fill a large pot 1-inch deep with water and bring to a boil. Add the mussels and boil gently until the shells just open, 5 to 7 minutes. Pour off half the liquid and keep rest of the liquid in the pot with the mussels. Discard any mussels that did not open. Add the wine, tomatoes, butter, garlic, basil, and shallots, and cook slowly on low heat (keep stirring occasionally) for about 20 minutes. Serve the mussels in a large bowl with hot crusty bread and salad.

*For plumper, more succulent mussels, place the mussels in a pot of cold water and stir in ½ cup flour; refrigerate for 4 hours or overnight. Drain the mussels and rinse in cold water.
**This may sound like too much garlic but it really isn't.

Baked Shrimp-Crab Salad

SERVES 6–8

1 green bell pepper, chopped
1 onion, chopped
1 cup finely chopped celery
One 6-ounce can crabmeat, picked
  free of any broken shells
One 4-ounce can medium shrimp

¾ cup mayonnaise
½ teaspoon salt
¼ teaspoon pepper
1 teaspoon Worcestershire sauce
1 cup buttered cracker crumbs or
  breadcrumbs

In a large bowl, combine the bell pepper, onion, and celery. Add the crabmeat and shrimp, then the mayonnaise and seasonings. Spoon the mixture into a buttered casserole, cover with buttered crumbs, and bake at 350 degrees until golden brown, about 30 minutes.

❧ ❧ ❧ *The Lady & Sons*

Tuna Burgers

SERVES 4

Two 6-ounce cans solid white
 tuna, drained
½ cup breadcrumbs
2 large eggs, lightly beaten
½ cup finely chopped onion
½ cup finely chopped celery
1 tablespoon chopped pimento
 (optional)

1 tablespoon fresh lemon juice
1½ teaspoons prepared horseradish
1 clove garlic, minced
¼ teaspoon pepper
1 tablespoon vegetable oil

In a large bowl, combine the tuna, breadcrumbs, and egg, and stir lightly. Add the onion, celery, pimento (if using), lemon juice, horse-radish, garlic, and pepper, and mix again. Form the mixture into four patties. Heat the oil in a nonstick skillet over medium heat and cook the patties, covered, until golden brown. Carefully flip the patties and cook the other side for 5 minutes.

Nootsie's Chesapeake Bay Crab Cakes

SERVES 4–6

½ cup peanut oil
1 pound crabmeat, picked free of
   any broken shells
1 egg
¼ cup dry breadcrumbs
4½ teaspoons heavy cream
2 tablespoons melted butter
2 tablespoons cracker crumbs

2 tablespoons chopped fresh parsley
2 tablespoons minced onion
1 teaspoon fresh lemon juice
½ teaspoon red pepper
½ teaspoon dry mustard
½ teaspoon salt
½ teaspoon Worcestershire sauce
¼ teaspoon black pepper

Pour the peanut oil into a large skillet and set aside. Combine all of the remaining ingredients and shape into 10 crab cakes. Heat the oil over medium-high heat, add the crab cakes (in batches), and fry until browned, 3 to 5 minutes. Flip the cakes and panfry the other side until golden brown.

Brandied Prime Rib

SERVES 6–8

8-pound standing rib roast
4–6 cloves garlic, slivered
¼ cup soy sauce
1 tablespoon freshly ground pepper

Fresh oregano and thyme sprigs
1 cup brandy
1 cup beef broth
Salt and pepper

Using a sharp knife, make 1-inch-deep slits, evenly spaced, over the entire surface of the roast; press the slivered garlic into the slits. Place in a roasting pan. Brush the outside of the roast with soy sauce, sprinkle with pepper and oregano and thyme sprigs, and let roast stand at room temperature for 1 hour.

    Preheat the oven to 350 degrees. Cook the roast to the preferred doneness: For medium rare, roast the beef 14 minutes per pound or until meat thermometer inserted into the center reads 125 degrees. For medium, roast 15 minutes per pound or until temperature reaches

135 degrees. While cooking, baste every 10 minutes with brandy. When the roast is done, transfer it to a warmed platter and let stand for 15 minutes before carving.

Skim and discard the fat from the roasting pan. Place the pan on the stove over medium heat and pour in the broth. Deglaze the pan by stirring to dislodge any browned bits. Simmer the sauce for a few minutes, then season with salt and pepper to taste. Carve the roast and spoon the sauce over the meat.

Ron's Grilled Peanut Butter Ham

SERVES 8–10

1 cup chicken broth
½ cup peanut butter
¼ cup honey
1 small onion, grated
1 clove garlic, chopped

2 teaspoons soy sauce
1 teaspoon Kitchen Bouquet
¼ teaspoon black pepper
2 center-cut ham slices (1½ inches thick)

In a blender, combine the broth, peanut butter, honey, onion, garlic, soy sauce, Kitchen Bouquet, and pepper. Put the ham in a shallow glass dish, pour the marinade over it, and marinate for 3 to 4 hours in the refrigerator.

Prepare a charcoal fire. Cook approximately 15 minutes per side over glowing coals. Carve into 1-inch-thick slices. This sauce is also excellent with lamb or pork chops.

Bubba's Country-Fried Venison Steak

SERVES 4

You may substitute beef round steak (have butcher run through cubing machine to tenderize) for venison if you like.

1½ cups, plus 2 tablespoons all-purpose flour
½ teaspoon black pepper
Eight 4-ounce venison steaks, cubed
1 teaspoon The Lady's House Seasoning
1 teaspoon The Lady's Seasoned Salt

¾ cup vegetable oil
1½ teaspoons salt
4 cups hot water
½ teaspoon Accent (optional)
1 bunch green onions, or 1 medium yellow onion, sliced

Combine 1½ cups flour and ¼ teaspoon of the black pepper. Sprinkle one side of meat with the House Seasoning and the other side with the Seasoned Salt. Dredge the meat in the flour mixture. Heat ½ cup oil in a heavy skillet over medium-high heat, add two of the venison steaks, and fry until nice and brown, 5 to 6 minutes per side. Repeat with the remaining steaks, adding up to ¼ cup oil, as needed.

When all the steaks are cooked, make the gravy: Add the 2 tablespoons of flour to the pan drippings; stir in the remaining ¼ teaspoon pepper, and the salt. Stir until the flour is medium brown and the mixture is bubbly. Slowly add the water and the Accent (if using), stirring constantly. Return the steaks to the skillet and bring to a boil; reduce the heat, place the onions on top of the steaks, cover, and simmer for 30 minutes.

Prince Charles' Calf's Liver

SERVES 4–6

Charles Polite is in charge of producing our evening buffet at The Lady &
Sons. I hold him in high esteem and therefore nicknamed him my "Prince
Charles." Our guests always enjoy his liver and onions. We hope you do as well.

1 cup (2 sticks) butter
1 jumbo onion, sliced
1½ pounds calf's liver
2 teaspoons The Lady's House
    Seasoning

2 teaspoons The Lady's Seasoned
    Salt
½ cup vegetable oil

In a large skillet, melt the butter over medium-high heat. Add the
onion and sauté until tender. Remove the onion and set aside; leave the
butter in the skillet. With a meat mallet, lightly pound the liver to tenderize it. Season the liver with House Seasoning and Seasoned Salt.
Add the oil to the skillet and heat until the oil crackles. Sear the liver
quickly on both sides. The liver is done when the surface is no longer
pink. Serve the liver topped with the onions.

    ❧ ❧ ❧   *The Lady & Sons*

Fried Veal

SERVES 4–6

2 pounds veal shoulder-blade steak
    (remove any bone and trim the
    fat)
¼ cup all-purpose flour
½ teaspoon salt
½ teaspoon garlic powder

¼ teaspoon pepper
2 eggs, lightly beaten
¾ cup seasoned breadcrumbs
4 tablespoons olive oil
1 cup water
½ pound sliced provolone cheese

Cut the veal into 8 individual size pieces. Dredge the meat in flour and
pound it with a meat mallet to half its original thickness. Sprinkle salt,

garlic powder, and pepper on both sides of the veal. Dip each piece into the beaten eggs, then into the breadcrumbs. Heat the oil in a large non-stick skillet over medium-high heat. Cook the veal pieces in batches until golden brown. Add the water, cover, and simmer for 45 minutes. Check the water level in the pan occasionally and add a little more water if necessary. Just before serving, place a slice of cheese on each piece of veal, cover the skillet, and serve as soon as the cheese melts.

Perfect Eye-of-Round Roast

SERVES 6–8

1 beef eye-of-round roast, 2½–3
   pounds
1 tablespoon vegetable oil
1 teaspoon The Lady's Seasoned
   Salt
1 teaspoon paprika

½ teaspoon sugar
½ teaspoon pepper
½ teaspoon garlic powder
¼ teaspoon dried oregano
¼ teaspoon ground ginger

Preheat the oven to 500 degrees. Rub the roast with oil. Mix all of the remaining ingredients in a small bowl. Completely coat all sides of roast with the seasonings. Place roast in a 12- to 15-inch iron skillet. Put the roast in the oven and immediately reduce the oven temperature to 350 degrees. Roast the beef for 20 minutes per pound. You may use a meat thermometer and cook to 125 degrees for medium-rare beef or 135–140 degrees for medium. Cool for 15 minutes before carving. Cut into thin slices across the grain of meat.

Spiced Beef with Dumplin's

SERVES 6–8

One 3-pound boneless chuck roast
2 tablespoons vegetable oil
One 16-ounce can tomatoes
1½ cups water

¼ cup red wine
2 teaspoons beef bouillon granules
1 teaspoon salt
¼ teaspoon pepper

2 cloves garlic, minced
6 whole cloves
1 package (8 count) refrigerated
  biscuits

1 tablespoon minced fresh parsley
¼ cup cold water
2 tablespoons cornstarch

Trim the excess fat from the roast. Heat the oil in a large Dutch oven over medium heat. Brown the roast on all sides. Add the tomatoes, water, wine, bouillon granules, salt, pepper, garlic, and cloves, cover, and cook slowly for 2 to 2½ hours, or until tender. Place the biscuits on the roast and sprinkle with parsley. Cover tightly and steam the dumplings for 15 minutes, giving the pot an occasional little shake. Remove the meat and dumplings to a platter. Make the gravy by mixing the water and cornstarch. Stir into the boiling broth, continuing to stir until the gravy is thick. (If the broth doesn't need thickening, you can serve it as is.)   ❧ ❧ ❧ *The Lady & Sons*

Sunday Morning Casserole

SERVES 6

2 slices white bread
1 pound ground mild sausage
6 eggs, beaten
2 cups milk
1 teaspoon dry mustard
½ teaspoon salt

Pinch of pepper
1½ cups thinly sliced, cooked,
  unpeeled red potatoes
1½ cups combined grated Cheddar
  and Monterey Jack cheeses

Cube the bread and place it in a buttered 8 × 11 × 2-inch casserole. Fry the sausage until it's almost done; drain off the fat. Mix the eggs, milk, dry mustard, salt, and pepper. Layer the sausage over the bread, and top with a layer of potatoes. Sprinkle the cheese on top. Pour the egg mixture over the casserole. Cover and refrigerate overnight. In the morning, bake the casserole at 350 degrees for 30 minutes or until set.

Baked Pasta Florentine

SERVES 8

One 10-ounce package frozen
   chopped spinach
1 tablespoon, plus ½ cup vegetable
   oil
1½ pounds ground beef
1 medium onion, chopped
1 clove garlic, minced
One 15½-ounce jar pasta sauce
   with mushrooms

One 8-ounce can tomato sauce
One 6-ounce can tomato paste
½ teaspoon salt
Pinch of pepper
1 8-ounce package seashell
   macaroni
1 cup shredded sharp cheese
½ cup breadcrumbs
2 eggs, well beaten

Cook the spinach according to package directions; drain, reserving the liquid and adding enough water to measure 1 cup; set aside. In a large, heavy pot, heat the 1 tablespoon of oil over medium heat. Brown the ground beef, onion, and garlic in the oil, stirring well to crumble the beef. Drain off the fat. Stir the spinach liquid, pasta sauce, tomato sauce, tomato paste, salt, and pepper into the meat mixture. Simmer for 10 minutes, then cover and set aside. Cook the macaroni according to package directions; drain and return the macaroni to the pot. Add the spinach, cheese, breadcrumbs, eggs, and the ½ cup of oil; stir gently to mix well. Spread the mixture evenly in a lightly greased 13½ × 8¾-inch baking dish. Top with the meat sauce and bake at 350 degrees for 30 minutes.   ❦ ❦ ❦ **The Lady & Sons**

Stuffed Red Peppers

SERVES 6–8

4 large red bell peppers, preferably
   with stems
¾ pound ground chuck
½ pound ground pork

1 medium onion, chopped
2 cloves garlic, minced
2 teaspoons beef bouillon
   granules

2 teaspoons The Lady's House
   Seasoning
1 cup cooked rice
½ cup jarred Old El Paso Cheese
   and Salsa

½ cup sour cream
1 cup diced tomatoes
½ cup chopped green onion tops
1 tablespoon soy sauce
1 cup hot water

Cut the peppers in half lengthwise, leaving the stems intact and halving them also. Remove the seeds and ribs. Sauté the beef and pork, the onion, garlic, 1 teaspoon of the bouillon granules, and the House Seasoning together, scrambling well, until the onion is transparent. Drain off the fat. Add the rice, cheese, sour cream, tomatoes, green onion tops, and soy sauce. Mix well. Stuff this mixture into peppers. Mix the hot water and the remaining 1 teaspoon bouillon granules. Pour this into a shallow casserole large enough to hold all the peppers. Place the stuffed peppers in the dish. (The water in the dish allows the peppers to steam while retaining some of their crispness.) Cover the casserole with foil and bake at 350 degrees for 25 to 35 minutes. Remove the foil and spoon a little juice over the peppers; bake for an additional 10 to 15 minutes.   ❧ ❧ ❧   *The Lady & Sons*

The Lady & Sons Smoked Boston Butt Roast

SERVES 12–15

The secret to this recipe is rubbing your seasonings into the meat thoroughly.

One 8-pound pork butt roast
4 tablespoons The Lady's House
   Seasoning
2 tablespoons The Lady's Seasoned
   Salt

4 tablespoons liquid smoke
1 medium onion, sliced
1 cup water
3 bay leaves

Sprinkle one side of the roast with 2 tablespoons of the House Seasoning, rubbing well. Flip the roast over and sprinkle with the remaining House Seasoning, rubbing well. Repeat the process with the Seasoned Salt and the liquid smoke. Place the meat in a large roaster pan; add the onion, water, and bay leaves. Cover and cook at 350 degrees for 2½ to

3 hours, or until a meat thermometer registers 170 degrees. Let cool slightly for easier slicing. Serve with a good barbecue sauce. Leftovers make wonderful chopped barbecue sandwiches.

❦ ❦ ❦ *The Lady & Sons*

Fried Spare Ribs

SERVES 4

When we serve fried ribs at the restaurant, the reaction is always the same: "Fried ribs, we've never heard of those!" Well, they really are very good. We all love fried pork chops, so why wouldn't we love fried ribs?

2 teaspoons The Lady's House
    Seasoning
½ teaspoon The Lady's Seasoned
    Salt

1 small slab pork ribs, 4–5 pounds
    (have the butcher crack them)
1 cup all-purpose flour
6 cups vegetable oil

Sprinkle the seasonings on both sides of the ribs, rubbing them thoroughly into the meat. Cut the slab into individual ribs. Roll each rib into flour, and shake off the excess. Drop the ribs, a few at a time, into hot, deep oil (350 degrees), and cook for 14 to 15 minutes. Drain on paper towels. Serve with barbecue sauce for dipping.

❦ ❦ ❦ *The Lady & Sons*

Duxelles-Stuffed Tenderloin

SERVES 8–12 AS AN ENTRÉE, 20–30 AS AN APPETIZER

DUXELLES
3 cups minced mushrooms
4 tablespoons butter
¼ cup-white wine
1 or 2 shallots, finely chopped
½ teaspoon salt
½ teaspoon pepper

MEAT
2 cups spinach
One 4–6-pound beef tenderloin,
    butterflied (ask the butcher to
    do this, or do it yourself)
1 tablespoon kosher salt
1 tablespoon minced garlic

6 ounces Gruyère cheese   ½ pound thinly sliced prosciutto
2 teaspoons pepper   2 tablespoons olive oil

For the duxelles, combine the mushrooms, butter, wine, shallots, salt, and pepper in a saucepan. Cook over medium-low heat until the mushrooms cook down and the liquid is completely evaporated. The duxelles can be made well in advance and refrigerated.

Place the spinach in a saucepan; sprinkle it with a few drops of water, cover, and cook over low heat just until the spinach is barely wilted. Drain and set aside.

Lay the beef on a flat surface and sprinkle it with 1½ teaspoons of the kosher salt; rub the garlic into the meat. Slice the cheese fairly thin and lay it on top of the meat, leaving a 2-inch border all around. Place the spinach on top of the cheese, followed by the duxelles, forming the filling into a long, narrow mound. Bring the sides of the meat together, overlapping the sides. Continue to shape and form the tenderloin to create a nice tight loaf. Sprinkle with the pepper and the remaining 1½ teaspoons kosher salt. Lay out the prosciutto on a large flat surface lined with waxed paper, forming a rectangle of prosciutto to accommodate the tenderloin. Lay the tenderloin on one end of the prosciutto slices and roll, using the waxed paper to help you. Roll until the prosciutto is snugly wrapped around the beef. Using 4 feet of cotton kitchen twine, tie one end of the tenderloin, then tie the meat much as you would lace your tennis shoes. Tie this on the snug side to allow for a little shrinkage of the meat. Drizzle olive oil over the meat, gently rubbing it over the entire roast. Bake in a preheated 450-degree oven for 45 minutes, or until a meat thermometer registers 140 degrees for medium-rare, 160 degrees for medium, and 170 degrees for well-done.

❧ ❧ ❧   *The Lady & Sons*

The Lady & Sons Pot Roast

SERVES 8

Before I give you this recipe, I must tell you a story. It is about a tall, handsome, talented young man who walked into our restaurant one hot Saturday afternoon. This beautiful young man had an equally beautiful and charming young woman on his arm. I could hear the wait staff just a'buzzing. Being ever watchful, I came out into the dining room to make sure all was well. I saw that our hostess had seated the couple, so I walked over and introduced myself and welcomed them to our home. That hot afternoon I had the pleasure of getting to know Harry Connick, Jr., and his lovely wife, Jill. I have Harry and Jill to thank for one of the most memorable nights of my life. Harry was performing that night at the Johnny Mercer Theater, but much to my dismay I had been too busy to get tickets. I laughingly told Harry that with the exception of him, just about everyone I cared to see in concert was dead, and because of my lack of organization I was going to miss this opportunity. With a sweet smile and a twinkle in his eye he said, "Well, I'm just not going on tonight if you're not going to be there." I repeated that I didn't have a ticket. Harry and Jill just smiled and said, "Yes you do. We'll have five tickets waiting at the box office for you and your two sons and their dates. Be there at 7:30." Shortly before show time Harry called the restaurant to see what was cooking. Well, every Saturday night we serve our wonderful Southern Pot Roast and Mashed Potatoes on the buffet. Harry's instructions were to put as much pot roast and mashed potatoes on one plate as we could, and to fill another plate with Jill's favorite, the collard greens. I was home getting ready to attend the concert when our manager, Renee, called to ask if I could pick the plates up on my way to the concert. I agreed, and said, "While you're fixing Harry's and Jill's plates, how about a platter of fried chicken and biscuits for the band members?" So my sons, their dates, and I, loaded down with food, took off for the concert. We had the pleasure of feeding the Connicks for a second time on that steaming hot day of August 21, 1999. The concert was wonderful! Harry left me speechless in the middle of his performance by recounting our meeting and describing the meals that he and Jill had enjoyed that day. Just when I thought he couldn't be sweeter, Harry dedicated his next song to me. The song was "Sensational." Needless to say, I was a puddle in my chair! Thank you, Harry and Jill, for a wonderful night. How proud your parents must be to have raised such gracious, thoughtful, considerate people. This one's for you, Harry!

One 3–4-pound boneless chuck
   roast
1 teaspoon The Lady's House
   Seasoning
1 teaspoon The Lady's Seasoned
   Salt
½ teaspoon black pepper
2 tablespoons vegetable oil

1 tablespoon beef bouillon granules
1 cup thinly sliced onion wedges
3 cloves garlic, crushed
2 bay leaves
One 10¾-ounce can cream of
   mushroom soup
¼ cup red wine
2 tablespoons Worcestershire sauce

Preheat the oven to 350 degrees. Rub the roast with House Seasoning, Seasoned Salt, and pepper. Heat the oil in a large skillet and brown the roast, searing it on both sides. Place the meat in a roaster pan. Sprinkle the bouillon granules over the meat, and cover it with onions, garlic, and bay leaves. Combine the mushroom soup, wine, Worcestershire sauce, and half a soup can of water, and pour this over the roast. Cover and bake for 2 to 2½ hours, or until tender. Remove and discard the bay leaves. If the gravy is not thick enough, remove the meat from the pan and pour the gravy into a saucepan. Bring it to a boil and thicken it by adding 2 tablespoons of cornstarch mixed with ¼ cup cold water, stirring constantly. ❦ ❦ ❦ *The Lady & Sons*

Roast Pork with Plum Sauce

SERVES 10

PLUM SAUCE
2 tablespoons butter
¾ cup chopped onions
1 cup plum preserves
⅔ cup water
½ cup packed brown sugar
⅓ cup chili sauce
¼ cup soy sauce
2 tablespoons prepared mustard
3 drops Tabasco sauce
2 tablespoons fresh lemon juice
Garlic salt to taste

ROAST
One 5-pound pork loin roast
2 cloves garlic, slivered
2 teaspoons salt
2 teaspoons dried or fresh rosemary
1½ teaspoons dried oregano
1½ teaspoons dried thyme
1½ teaspoons rubbed sage
¼ teaspoon pepper
¼ teaspoon freshly grated nutmeg

To make the saucce, melt the butter in a saucepan; add the onions and sauté until tender. Add the remaining ingredients and simmer for 15 minutes. Set aside.

Preheat the oven to 325 degrees. Moisten the roast with a damp paper towel to help hold the seasonings. In a small bowl, stir together the garlic, salt, herbs, and spices. With a sharp knife make ½-inch-deep slits in the top of the roast. Press the seasoning mixture into the slits, and rub the remainder over the entire roast. Place the roast in a roaster pan and pour ½ cup plum sauce over it. Cover and bake for 2½ hours. Uncover the roast and baste it with additional plum sauce; bake for 30 minutes longer, basting 2 or 3 times, until the roast is nicely browned. Serve the remaining plum sauce on the side for dipping.

Baked Spaghetti

SERVES 10

Dora Charles—my head cook, my soul sister, and my friend—really puts her big toe in this dish. In fact, Fodor's Travel Guide *called it "The Best Baked Spaghetti in the South." Go, Dora! (P.S. Dora doesn't really put her toe in this, that's just a Southern expression we use when someone has done a dish just right!)*

2 cups canned diced tomatoes	1½ teaspoon The Lady's Seasoned
2 cups tomato sauce	Salt
1 cup water	1½ teaspoons sugar
½ cup diced onions	2 small bay leaves
½ cup diced green bell peppers	1½ pounds ground beef
2 cloves garlic, chopped	8 ounces uncooked angelhair pasta
¼ cup chopped fresh parsley	1 cup grated Cheddar cheese
1½ teaspoons Italian seasoning	1 cup grated Monterey Jack cheese
1½ teaspoons The Lady's House	
Seasoning	

To make the sauce, in a stockpot, combine the tomatoes, tomato sauce, water, onions, peppers, garlic, parsley, seasoning mixtures, sugar, and bay leaves. Bring to a boil, then reduce the heat and simmer, covered, for 1 hour. Crumble the ground beef in a saucepan. Cook until no pink remains, then drain off the fat. Add the ground beef to the stockpot. Simmer for another 20 minutes. While the sauce simmers, cook the pasta according to the package directions. Cover the bottom of a 13 × 9 × 2-inch pan with sauce. Add a layer of pasta, then half of the cheese; repeat the layers, ending with the sauce. Bake at 350 degrees for 30 minutes. Top with the remaining cheese, return to the oven, and continue to cook until the cheese is melted and bubbly. Cut into squares before serving. ❦ ❦ ❦ *The Lady & Sons*

Pepper Steak

SERVES 4–6

¼ cup vegetable oil
1½ pounds round steak, trimmed
  of fat and cut in strips
1 cup water
1 medium onion, sliced
½ teaspoon garlic salt
¼ teaspoon ground ginger

2 medium green bell peppers, cut
  into strips
2 tablespoons soy sauce
2–3 teaspoons sugar
1 tablespoon cornstarch
2 tomatoes, cut into wedges

Heat the oil in a large, heavy pot. Add the meat and brown for 5 minutes. Stir in the water, onion, garlic salt, and ginger. Bring to a boil, cover, reduce the heat, and simmer for 15 minutes. After 10 minutes, add the peppers. Stir together the soy sauce, sugar, and cornstarch. Pour this into the pot and stir until the liquid thickens. Place tomato wedges on top of the meat and bring to a boil. Simmer for 5 minutes longer. Serve over rice. ❧ ❧ ❧ **The Lady & Sons**

Venison Wellington with Oyster Pâté

SERVES 4

1½–2 pounds venison tenderloin
  (backstrap works, too)
Salt and pepper
Vegetable oil
1 tablespoon butter
2 ounces peeled shallots, finely
  chopped
1 clove garlic, finely chopped
4 ounces mushrooms, finely
  chopped

12 ounces shucked May River
  Oysters (or the best oysters
  available in your area),
  drained of liquor and picked
  free of any broken shells
1 tablespoon dry sherry
2 tablespoons fresh breadcrumbs
Sour Cream Pastry (recipe
  follows)
1 egg, beaten with 1 teaspoon
  water

Preheat the oven to 450 degrees. Rub the tenderloin with salt and pepper and brush it lightly with oil. Heat a skillet over medium-high heat and lightly sear all surfaces of the meat, including the ends. Remove the meat from the pan and set aside. Melt the butter over high heat; add the shallots and garlic and sauté for 2 to 3 minutes. Add the mushrooms and sauté for 2 to 3 minutes longer. Add the oysters and sherry, and cook until the oysters are opaque. Remove from the heat and allow to cool slightly. Drain off any liquid and combine the mixture with the breadcrumbs in the bowl of a food processor. Process until well blended and nearly smooth. Line a colander with several layers of cheesecloth and spoon the pâté into it. Allow to drain for 10 to 15 minutes. If the pâté seems too wet, pick up the edge of the cheesecloth, twist it together, and wring out the excess liquid.

Roll the pastry dough out on a lightly floured surface to form a rectangle less than ¼ inch thick. Spoon some pâté into the center of the dough and spread it to form a shape similar to that of the tenderloin. Place the venison on the pâté, then cover the top and sides of the meat with the remaining pâté. Wrap the pastry around the venison, overlapping the edges to form a seam. Moisten the edges with water and pinch lightly to seal. Trim the top layer of pastry from both ends and fold the ends up over the sides of the venison, sealing as before. Carefully turn over the pastry-wrapped tenderloin and place seam-side down on a lightly greased baking sheet. Brush with the beaten egg. Decorate the top with designs cut from the pastry scraps. Brush the cutouts with beaten egg. Bake the tenderloin for 15 to 20 minutes, or until the pastry is golden brown. Remove from the oven and let stand in a warm place for 10 minutes before carving.

VARIATIONS: For those who don't care for oysters, a mushroom duxelles may be used instead of pâté. Substitute 8 ounces of finely chopped fresh mushrooms (any kind will do) for the oysters, and follow the above procedure. You may also substitute a beef tenderloin for the venison.

SOUR CREAM PASTRY

1½ cups all-purpose flour   *½ cup sour cream*
½ teaspoon salt
¾ cup (1½ sticks) unsalted butter,
  chilled

Combine the flour and salt in a food processor and pulse once or twice
to mix. Cut the butter into chunks and add it to the processor. Process
until the mixture resembles coarse cornmeal. Add the sour cream and
pulse until the dough forms a ball. Remove the dough and knead it a
few times. Wrap the dough in waxed paper and refrigerate for at least
1 hour. The dough can be frozen for up to 1 month; allow it to thaw
partially before rolling.

Wayne's Beef Macaroni and Cheese

SERVES 8–10

One 1-pound box elbow macaroni   *3 cups canned crushed tomatoes*
2 tablespoons vegetable oil   *Salt and pepper*
2 cups chopped green bell pepper   *1 teaspoon each dried basil,*
2 cups chopped onion   *cumin, and dried oregano*
1 tablespoon chopped garlic   *2–3 cups grated Cheddar cheese*
2 pounds lean ground beef

Cook the macaroni according to package directions; drain and set
aside. Heat the oil in a skillet; add the peppers, onion, and garlic, and
sauté until soft. Add the ground beef and sauté until browned. Add the
tomatoes, salt and pepper to taste, and the basil, cumin, and oregano.
In a large bowl, combine the macaroni and the beef mixture. Spread
this mixture in a 9 × 13-inch baking dish. Top with the cheese and
bake at 350 degrees for 20 to 25 minutes, or until the cheese is lightly
browned and bubbly. Ground turkey or chicken can be used in place of
beef, if desired.

The Lady's Pork Stew

SERVES 8–10

One 3-pound Boston butt roast, trimmed of exterior fat

2 tablespoons Dale's Steak Seasoning

1½ teaspoons The Lady's House Seasoning

1½ teaspoons The Lady's Seasoned Salt

1 teaspoon garlic salt

2 tablespoons vegetable oil

6 cups water

1 medium onion, cut into wedges

2 bay leaves

Salt and pepper

1½ cups sliced carrots

3 medium turnips, skin on, cut into wedges

3 medium red potatoes, skin on, cut into wedges

3 tablespoons cornstarch

⅓ cup cold water

Rub the meat well with the Dale's Seasoning, House Seasoning, Seasoned Salt, and garlic salt—in that order. If time allows, let the roast sit for 1 hour at room temperature. Heat the oil in a Dutch oven. Cook the roast on all sides until browned. Add the 6 cups of water, the onion, and the bay leaves. Bring to a boil, reduce the heat, cover, and simmer for 1½ to 2 hours. Remove the meat from the pot and allow to cool. Cut the pork into chunks. While meat is cooling, taste the stock and add salt and pepper, if necessary. Add the carrots, turnips, and potatoes to the Dutch oven and return to a boil. Cover, reduce the heat, and cook for 15 minutes or until the vegetables are tender. Stir the cornstarch into the ⅓ cup water. Pour this into the pot and stir until the liquid thickens. Return the pork to the pot and simmer for 10 to 15 minutes longer. ❦ ❦ ❦ *The Lady & Sons*

St. Paddy's Day Corned Beef and Cabbage

SERVES 8

Savannah holds the second largest St. Patrick's Day celebration in the United States. It is quite a sight to see: Our city turns green and corned beef and cabbage is everyone's favorite dish for the day.

One 3-pound corned beef brisket
1 large head green cabbage*
4–6 tablespoons butter

1–2 teaspoons The Lady's House
Seasoning

Place the corned beef in a large stockpot and cover it with cold water to nearly fill pot. Some corned beef comes with a sealed packet of seasoning. If yours does, add it to the pot. Bring to a boil, reduce the heat, cover, and simmer for 2½ to 3 hours, or until the beef is firm but tender to the fork. Remove the beef from the pot. When the corned beef is almost done, chop the cabbage. (If it has a lot of outside dark green leaves, chop them separately and set aside. These leaves add beautiful color to the dish, but they are tougher and require a little more cooking time, so put them in the pot about 10 minutes before you add the remaining cabbage.) Place the cabbage in a colander and rinse it with cool water. When you are ready to add the cabbage, in a separate pot, melt the butter over medium-high heat. Immediately add the cabbage to the pot, leaving as much water as possible on the leaves. Cook, stirring until the cabbage is well coated with butter. Sprinkle with the House Seasoning. Cover the pot and simmer until the cabbage is tender but still somewhat crisp, 7 to 10 minutes.

Slice the corned beef thinly across the grain. Place the cabbage in a serving dish and place the sliced corned beef on top. You can drizzle a spoonful or two of stock from the pot over the corned beef and cabbage, if you like. Serve with mashed potatoes and Corny Corn Muffins (see page 136). Leftover corned beef makes wonderful sandwiches.

❦ ❦ ❦ *The Lady & Sons*

*When we're serving cabbage without the corned beef, we season the pot with a little bacon along with the butter: Fry 2 to 3 strips of cut-up bacon along with the butter until the bacon is about half done, then proceed with the recipe.

Sausage with Ravishing Rice

SERVES 10–12

1 pound fresh sausage
5 cups water
1 cup raw long-grain white rice
2 packages dry chicken noodle soup
   mix from a 4.2-ounce box
1 cup chopped onion
1 large green bell pepper, chopped
1 cup finely chopped celery

¼ cup (½ stick) butter
½ teaspoon The Lady's Seasoned
   Salt
1 teaspoon The Lady's House
   Seasoning
¼ cup chopped fresh parsley
¼ cup slivered almonds
⅛ teaspoon paprika

Preheat the oven to 350 degrees. Crumble the sausage and cook in a skillet over medium heat until nicely browned; drain well and set aside. In a large, heavy pot, bring the water to a boil, add the rice and soup mix, and cook for 10 minutes, stirring occasionally. Add the sausage, onion, bell pepper, celery, butter, seasonings, and parsley. Pour into a greased 2-quart casserole, top with almonds, and sprinkle with paprika. Bake the casserole for 40 to 50 minutes, or until all liquid is absorbed.

Dixieland Pork Chops

SERVES 4–8

1½–2 pounds thin pork chops (8
   chops)
½ cup all-purpose flour
3 tablespoons vegetable oil
½ cup chopped onions
1 clove garlic, minced
One 10¾-ounce can Cheddar
   cheese soup

One 7-ounce can broiled
   mushrooms with broth
1 tablespoon Worcestershire sauce
1 teaspoon The Lady's House
   Seasoning

Dredge the pork chops in the flour. Reserve the excess flour. Heat the oil in a large skillet, add two or three chops, and brown them on both sides until half done. Repeat with the remaining chops. Remove the meat from the skillet and add the onions and garlic (if necessary, add a little more oil to the pan). Sauté until the onions are golden. Sprinkle the reserved flour over the onions and stir until blended. Add the soup, mushrooms, Worcestershire sauce, and House Seasoning. Simmer, stirring, until the sauce is hot and bubbly. Place a layer of pork chops in a 13 × 9 × 2-inch casserole; pour half the sauce over the chops, then add another layer of chops, and top with the remaining sauce. Bake at 275 degrees for an hour and a half, until the pork chops are tender. Serve over hot creamy grits, white rice, or egg noodles.

❦ ❦ ❦ *The Lady & Sons*

Barbecued Short Ribs

SERVES 4

2 pounds short ribs, cut in 2-inch
   pieces
Salt
¼ cup minced onion
½ cup ketchup
¼ cup water

2 tablespoons fresh lemon juice
2 tablespoons brown sugar
1 tablespoon prepared mustard
⅛ teaspoon salt
1 tablespoon Worcestershire sauce

Trim the top layer of fat from the short ribs. Place several pieces of this fat in a Dutch oven, and cook over medium heat until the bottom is lightly coated with fat. Remove the pot from the heat. Sprinkle the short ribs with salt, then brown them on all sides, removing pieces as they are done. Add the onion and sauté until lightly browned. Return the short ribs to the pot and add the ketchup, water, lemon juice, sugar, mustard, salt, and Worcestershire sauce. Cover the pot and cook over low heat for 2 hours, or until tender, stirring occasionally. Or, you may finish cooking the short ribs in the covered pot in a 300-degree oven.

Texas-Style Chili

YIELDS ABOUT 5 QUARTS

3 pounds ground chuck
1 pound hot bulk sausage
3 medium onions, chopped
4 cloves garlic, minced
¼ cup chili powder
2 tablespoons all-purpose flour
1 tablespoon sugar

1 tablespoon dried oregano
1 teaspoon salt
Two 28-ounce cans whole tomatoes,
*   chopped, with their juice*
Three 16-ounce cans kidney beans,
*   or Bush's hot chili beans,*
*   drained*

Combine the ground chuck, sausage, onions, and garlic in a Dutch oven. Cook over medium heat until the meat is browned; stir the meat to break it up as it cooks. Drain off the pan drippings. Stir in chili powder, flour, sugar, oregano, and salt, and stir well to mix. Cover, and simmer for 1 hour, stirring occasionally. Add the tomatoes, beans, and simmer for 20 minutes longer.   ❦ ❦ ❦ **The Lady & Sons**

Ron's Tybee Island Sausage Pie

SERVES 6

1 pound ground sausage
1 tablespoon butter
⅓ cup chopped onion
¾ cup milk
One 3-ounce package cream cheese
3 eggs
1 cup shredded Cheddar cheese

½ teaspoon Worcestershire sauce
½ teaspoon salt (use less if the
*   sausage is salty)*
⅛ teaspoon pepper
One 9-inch deep-dish pie crust,
*   partially baked and cooled*

Preheat the oven to 375 degrees. In a heavy skillet over medium heat, crumble the sausage with a fork. Sauté the sausage until completely cooked. Drain off the fat, remove the sausage, and set aside. Melt the butter in another skillet over medium heat. Sauté the onions in the butter until tender. Add the milk and heat until steam rises, but do not boil the milk. Cut the cream cheese into small pieces, add it to the onion mixture, and remove the pan from the heat. In a large bowl, beat the eggs, then add the Cheddar, the onion mixture, the Worcestershire, salt, and pepper. Mix thoroughly and pour this into the pie crust. Top with cooked sausage, and bake for 30 minutes, or until set.

Steak Diane

SERVES 4

6 tablespoons butter	*1 teaspoon Worcestershire sauce*
½ cup sliced mushrooms	*⅛ teaspoon salt*
2 tablespoons minced onion	*2 tablespoons snipped fresh parsley*
1 clove garlic, crushed	*1 pound beef tenderloin, cut into 8*
1 teaspoon fresh lemon juice	*slices*

Melt 4 tablespoons of the butter in a large skillet over medium heat. Add the mushrooms, onions, garlic, lemon juice, Worcestershire sauce, and salt, and cook, stirring, until the mushrooms are tender. Stir in the parsley; pour the sauce into a small metal bowl or saucepan, cover, and keep warm. Melt the remaining 2 tablespoons of butter in the skillet. Cook the steaks over medium-high heat, turning them once, for 3 to 4 minutes on each side for medium. Serve the steaks with the mushroom sauce.

Barbecue Meat Loaf

SERVES 6

1½ pounds ground beef	*Two 8-ounce cans tomato sauce*
1 cup fresh breadcrumbs	*½ cup water*
1 onion, chopped	*3 tablespoons vinegar*
1 egg, lightly beaten	*3 tablespoons brown sugar*
1½ teaspoons salt	*2 tablespoons prepared mustard*
½ teaspoon pepper	*2 tablespoons Worcestershire sauce*

Mix together the beef, breadcrumbs, onion, egg, salt, pepper, and ½ cup of the tomato sauce. Form this mixture into a loaf and place it in a shallow pan. Stir together the remaining tomato sauce, the water, vinegar, sugar, mustard, and Worcestershire. Pour this sauce over the meatloaf. Bake at 350 degrees for 1 hour, basting occasionally with the pan juices.   ❧ ❧ ❧ **The Lady & Sons**

Perfect Char-Grilled Filet Mignon

SERVES 2

One 8-ounce bottle zesty Italian
   salad dressing
2 beef tenderloin fillets,
   1½–2 inches thick

2 slices bacon
2 tablespoons Lea and Perrins
   Steak Sauce
2 teaspoons water

Pour the salad dressing into a shallow pan, place the steaks in the pan, and let them marinate for 3 to 4 hours.

Prepare a fire in a charcoal grill. Wrap a strip of bacon around each steak, securing it with a toothpick. Grill the steaks over hot coals for about 8 minutes per side (5 minutes per side for rare). Baste with a mixture of steak sauce and water. For perfect steaks, turn them only once.

Hot Savannah Chicken Salad Casserole

SERVES 8–10

Two 10¾-ounce cans condensed
   cream of chicken soup
1½ cups mayonnaise
1 tablespoon prepared mustard
1 tablespoon Worcestershire sauce
One 10-ounce bag potato chips,
   crushed

½ cup slivered almonds
4 cups cubed cooked chicken
2 cups diced celery
¼ cup finely chopped onion
4 hard-boiled eggs, sliced

Lightly butter a 13 × 9 × 2-inch casserole. Stir together the soup, mayonnaise, mustard, and Worcestershire sauce. In a medium bowl, reserve 1 cup of the potato chips and 2 tablespoons of the almonds for the topping. Place half of the remaining potato chips in the casserole, spreading them evenly. Place half each of the chicken, celery, onion, eggs, and remaining almonds in the casserole, then spread half of the soup mixture on top. Repeat the layers, ending with the reserved potato chips and almonds. Bake at 350 degrees for 30 to 40 minutes, or until heated through.

Mexican Chicken

SERVES 8

One 10¾-ounce can cream of
   chicken soup
One 10¾-ounce can Cheddar
   cheese soup
One 10¾-ounce can cream of
   mushroom soup
One 10-ounce can Ro-Tel
   tomatoes

1 whole chicken, cooked, boned,
   and chopped, or 4 cups leftover
   cooked chicken
One 11½-ounce package flour
   tortillas
2 cups shredded Cheddar cheese

In a large bowl, stir together the three kinds of soup and the tomatoes. Stir in the chicken. In a greased 13 × 9-inch pan, layer the tortillas and the chicken mixture, beginning and ending with tortillas. Sprinkle the cheese over the casserole and bake at 350 degrees for 30 minutes.

❦ ❦ ❦   *The Lady & Sons*

Hurry-Up Chicken Pot Pie

SERVES 4–6

This casual dish is a shortcut version of the lavish Chicken Pot Pie on our dinner menu.

2 cups chopped cooked chicken
breast
2 hard-boiled eggs, sliced
½ cup thinly sliced carrots
½ cup frozen green peas
1 cup chicken broth

One 10¾-ounce can cream of
chicken soup
Salt and pepper (optional)
1 cup Lady & Sons Biscuit Mix
1 cup milk
½ cup (1 stick) melted butter

In a greased 2-quart casserole, layer the chicken, eggs, carrots, and peas. Mix the broth with the soup, and season with salt and pepper, if desired. Pour over the layers. Stir together the Biscuit Mix and milk, and pour this over the casserole. Drizzle butter over the topping. Bake at 350 degrees until the topping is golden brown, 30 to 40 minutes.

❦ ❦ ❦ *The Lady & Sons*

Quail with Marsala Sauce

SERVES 8 AS AN APPETIZER, 4 AS A MAIN DISH

4 slices bacon
4–8 dressed quail
Salt and pepper
1 tablespoon olive oil
1 tablespoon butter
8 ounces fresh mushrooms, sliced
2 ounces shallots, minced

1 clove garlic, minced
1 tablespoon all-purpose flour
1¼ cups chicken broth
3 ounces Marsala
½ cup sour cream
1½ cups cooked white rice
1½ cups cooked wild rice

In a large skillet, cook the bacon over medium heat until crisp; crumble the bacon and set aside. Drain all but 1 tablespoon bacon fat from the pan. Rub the quail with salt and pepper, and brown them on all sides in the skillet over medium-high heat. Place the quail in a single layer in a 13 × 9-inch casserole. Add the oil and butter to the pan. Over medium heat, add the mushrooms, shallots, and garlic; sauté until the mushrooms begin to release their liquid. Remove the mushrooms from the pan with a slotted spoon and put them in the casserole. Stir the flour into the hot fat in the pan and cook, stirring until the roux begins to bubble and brown (take care not to burn it). Add the broth and Marsala; when the mixture begins to thicken, remove the pan from the heat and whisk in the sour cream. Pour the sauce over the quail and mushrooms. Bake in a 350-degree oven until the sauce is bubbly and quail has cooked through, 15 to 20 minutes. Combine the white rice and wild rice in a bowl and keep warm. Serve the quail on a bed of rice with the Marsala sauce and mushrooms spooned on top.

Chicken with Drop Dumplin's

SERVES 6–8

One 3–4-pound chicken, cut up
2 stalks celery, diced
2 tablespoons chicken bouillon
   granules
1 bay leaf
8 cups water
2 cups all-purpose flour
4 teaspoons baking powder
1 teaspoon salt

¾ cup milk
½ cup green onion tops, chopped
Pinch of cayenne pepper
½ cup chopped fresh parsley
¼ teaspoon freshly grated nutmeg
One 10¾-ounce can cream of
   chicken soup
Salt and pepper

Place the chicken pieces, celery, bouillon granules, and bay leaf in a stockpot. Add the water and bring to a boil over medium-high heat. Reduce the heat and cook for 45 minutes to 1 hour, or until the chicken is tender. Remove the chicken and let it cool slightly. Pick the meat off of the bones, discarding the bones and skin; set aside.

Sift the flour, baking powder, and salt into a large bowl. Add the milk and mix well. Add the onions and cayenne, and mix. Drop the batter by tablespoons into the boiling broth until all the batter is used up. Gently shake the pot. (Never stir dumplings with a spoon, as this will tear them up.) Add the parsley and nutmeg, and shake the pot again. Cover, reduce the heat, and simmer gently for about 15 minutes without lifting the lid.

While the dumplings are cooking, heat the soup with 1 can of water in a small saucepan. When the dumplings are done, carefully pour the soup into the dumpling pot. Shake the pot gently. Return the chicken to the pot and again shake the pot, this time in a rotating motion. Season to taste with salt and pepper.

❧ ❧ ❧ **The Lady & Sons**

Basil Grilled Chicken

SERVES 4

¾ teaspoon coarsely ground black
  pepper
4 skinned chicken breast halves
¼ cup chopped fresh basil, plus 2
  tablespoons minced fresh basil
⅓ cup (5 tablespoons) butter,
  melted, plus ½ cup (1 stick)
  butter, at room temperature

1 tablespoon grated Parmesan
¼ teaspoon garlic powder
⅛ teaspoon salt
⅛ teaspoon pepper
Fresh basil sprigs (optional)

Prepare a fire in a charcoal grill. Press the coarsely ground pepper into the meaty side of the chicken breast halves. Stir the chopped basil into the melted butter. Brush the chicken lightly with this mixture. In a small bowl, combine the softened butter, minced basil, Parmesan, garlic powder, salt, and pepper. Beat at low speed with an electric mixer until smoothly blended. Transfer to a small serving bowl; set aside.

Grill the chicken over medium coals for 8 to 10 minutes on each side, basting frequently with the remaining melted butter mixture.

Serve the grilled chicken with the basil-butter mixture. Garnish with fresh basil sprigs if desired.

Chicken Bog

SERVES 10–12

One 3-pound chicken, quartered
1 pound smoked link sausage
1 cup chopped onion
½ cup (1 stick) butter

2 teaspoons The Lady's Seasoned
  Salt
2 teaspoons The Lady's House
  Seasoning

1 teaspoon ground red pepper
1 teaspoon ground black pepper
3 bay leaves

8 cups water
3 cups raw white rice

Slice the sausage into ½-inch pieces. In a stockpot, combine the chicken, sausage, onion, butter, and seasonings. Add the water, bring to a boil, cover, and cook at a low boil for 40 minutes. Remove the chicken from the pot and let cool slightly. Pick the meat from the bones, discarding the bones and skin. Add the rice to the pot and bring to a boil, stirring well. Boil for 10 minutes, then reduce the heat, cover the pot, and simmer for 10 minutes, or until the rice is done. Remove the bay leaves, and return the chicken to the pot.

❧ ❧ ❧ *The Lady & Sons*

Chicken Casserole

SERVES 6

2 cups cubed cooked chicken
2 cups breadcrumbs
1 cup cooked rice
1 cup milk
One 2-ounce jar pimentos, finely
   chopped
1½ teaspoons salt

Pinch of cayenne pepper
4 eggs, well beaten
One 10¾-ounce can cream of
   mushroom soup
1 cup heavy cream

In a large bowl, combine the chicken, breadcrumbs, rice, milk, pimentos, salt, and cayenne. Stir in the eggs. Pour the mixture into a buttered 2-quart baking dish and bake at 325 degrees for 1 hour. For the sauce, in a small saucepan stir together the soup and cream and heat until bubbly. Serve the sauce on the side. ❧ ❧ ❧ *The Lady & Sons*

Fricasé de Pollo

SERVES 4

4 boneless chicken breast halves
1 large tomato, peeled and diced
2 cloves garlic, minced
2 bay leaves
1 teaspoon dried oregano
¼ teaspoon black pepper
½ cup white wine
One 8-ounce can tomato sauce

1 medium onion, diced
12 pitted green olives
1 tablespoon capers
1½ teaspoons olive oil
1 green bell pepper, sliced
Salt
One 2-ounce jar pimentos

Put all the ingredients except the pimentos in a Dutch oven on top of the stove. Over medium heat, bring to a boil. Reduce the heat and cook until the chicken is tender. Stir in the pimentos. Serve the fricasé over rice.

Chicken Boudine

SERVES 8–10

2 cups freshly cooked egg noodles
Two 10¾-ounce cans cream of
    mushroom soup
½ cup chicken broth
¼ cup dry sherry
4 cups chopped cooked chicken
3 cups grated sharp cheese

One 2¼-ounce package slivered
    almonds, toasted
½ cup drained, chopped pimentos
One 4-ounce can sliced
    mushrooms, drained
Salt and pepper

In a large bowl, toss together the noodles, soup, broth, and sherry. Add the chicken, 2 cups of the cheese, the almonds, pimento, mushrooms, and salt and pepper to taste, and toss gently to combine. Transfer the mixture to a greased 13 × 9 × 2-inch casserole and top with the remaining cup of cheese.

Bake at 350 degrees for 30 minutes, or until bubbly.

Chicken Florentine

SERVES 6–8

Two 10-ounce packages frozen
  spinach (or chopped broccoli)
Two 10¾-ounce cans cream of
  mushroom soup
1 cup mayonnaise
1 cup sour cream
1 cup grated sharp Cheddar cheese
¼ cup white wine or sherry

1 tablespoon fresh lemon juice
1 teaspoon curry powder
Salt and pepper
6 cooked chicken breast halves,
  shredded
½ cup grated Parmesan
½ cup breadcrumbs

Cook and drain the spinach; set aside. In a large bowl, mix together the soup, mayonnaise, sour cream, Cheddar, wine, lemon juice, curry powder, and salt and pepper to taste. Spread the chicken in a greased 13 × 9-inch casserole. Cover the chicken with spinach, then pour the soup mixture over the spinach. Combine the Parmesan and breadcrumbs and sprinkle this over the casserole. Bake at 350 degrees for 30 minutes.

Pat's Almond Chicken Casserole

SERVES 8–10

This casserole can be prepared in advance and refrigerated or frozen. Thaw the frozen casserole in the refrigerator overnight before baking.

8 boneless chicken breast halves
One 2¼-ounce package sliced
  almonds
One 10¾-ounce can cream of
  celery soup
One 10¾-ounce can cream of
  chicken soup

One 10¾-ounce can cream of
  mushroom soup
1 cup sour cream
½ cup chopped celery
3 tubes Ritz Crackers, crushed
¾ cup (1½ sticks) melted butter

Place the chicken in a large, deep skillet and add water to cover. Cook over medium heat for 30 minutes, or until tender.

Meanwhile, place the almonds in a shallow pan and toast in a 300-degree oven for 5 minutes, or until pale golden brown. Watch closely—almonds can scorch quickly. Tip the almonds into a plate and set aside.

Drain and cool the chicken and tear it into bite-size pieces. Put the chicken in a large bowl and add the three cans of soup, the sour cream, and the celery; mix well. Spread the chicken mixture in a greased 13 × 9-inch pan. Mix the crackers and butter, and cover the casserole with the crumbs. Bake at 350 degrees for 30 minutes, or until bubbly.

Saucy Chicken and Asparagus Bake

SERVES 4

1½ pounds fresh asparagus spears, trimmed and halved
2 tablespoons vegetable oil
4 boneless chicken breast halves
½ teaspoon salt
¼ teaspoon pepper

One 10¾-ounce can cream of chicken soup
½ cup mayonnaise
1 teaspoon fresh lemon juice
1 cup shredded Cheddar cheese

If the asparagus spears are thick or seem tough, cook them in boiling water for 2 minutes; drain. Place the asparagus in a greased 9 × 9-inch baking dish. Heat the oil in a skillet over medium heat; add the chicken and brown on both sides; season with salt and pepper. Arrange the chicken over the asparagus. In a bowl, mix the soup, mayonnaise, and lemon juice; pour this over the chicken. Cover and bake at 375 degrees for 40 minutes, or until the chicken is tender and its juices run clear. Sprinkle the dish with the cheese and let stand for 5 minutes so the cheese melts.   ❦ ❦ ❦ *The Lady & Sons*

Szechuan Chicken with Angelhair Pasta

SERVES 4

1 tablespoon dark sesame oil
¼ cup chili-garlic sauce (found in the Asian section of your grocery store)
4 boneless chicken breast halves
1 pound angelhair pasta
1½ pounds broccoli crowns, cut into florets
1 red bell pepper, cut into ½-inch strips
1 yellow bell pepper, cut into ½-inch strips
12 green onions
2 cloves garlic, minced
¼ cup soy sauce
1½ teaspoons minced fresh ginger

Heat the oil and 2 tablespoons of the chili-garlic sauce in a large skillet over medium heat; add the chicken, and cook for 4 minutes on each side, or until cooked through. Meanwhile bring a large pot of water to a boil for pasta. Add pasta to boiling water, cook as directed on package, and drain. Remove the chicken from the pan and cut it into strips. Add the broccoli, bell peppers, green onions, garlic, remaining chili-garlic sauce, soy sauce, and ginger to the skillet. Cook the vegetables, stirring until they are crisp-tender. Add the chicken strips and cook until heated through. Serve over the pasta.

Savannah Gumbo

SERVES 10–12

2 tablespoons all-purpose flour
2 tablespoons butter
1 onion, chopped
1 green bell pepper, chopped
1 tablespoon chopped garlic (2–3 cloves)
2 cups diced or sliced smoked sausage
4 large boneless chicken breasts, diced
4 cups chicken broth
One 28-ounce can diced tomatoes
2 cups cut okra
1 teaspoon dried thyme
2 bay leaves
½ teaspoon cayenne pepper
1 teaspoon filé powder
Salt and pepper

In a 5-quart pot combine the flour and butter and cook over medium heat, stirring constantly, until the roux has browned to a light chocolate color. Add the onion, pepper, and garlic, and sauté for 2 minutes. Add the sausage, chicken, broth, tomatoes, okra, thyme, bay leaves, and cayenne, and simmer over low heat for 45 to 50 minutes. Add the filé powder and salt and pepper to taste. Remove and discard the bay leaves. Serve the gumbo over rice. For an extra special pot of gumbo, throw in some peeled shrimp before adding the filé.

❦ ❦ ❦ *The Lady & Sons*

Chicken and Wild Rice Casserole

SERVES 8

One 6-ounce package long-grain
  and wild rice, cooked according
  to directions
4 cups diced cooked chicken breast
Two 10¾-ounce cans cream of
  chicken soup

1 cup mayonnaise
2 teaspoons curry powder, or to
  taste
One 8-ounce package Pepperidge
  Farm Cornbread Dressing Mix
¼ cup (½ stick) butter

Put the rice in a greased 2-quart casserole. Layer the chicken on top of the rice. Mix the soup, mayonnaise, and curry powder, and pour this over the chicken. Sprinkle the dressing mix over the casserole and dot with butter. Bake at 350 degrees for 30 minutes or until bubbly.

Vegetables and Side Dishes

Fancy Green Beans

Sweet Potato Casserole

Southern-Style Black-Eyed Peas

Tomato Casserole

Saturday Night Vidalia Onions

Corn Casserole

Jelly Roll's Crab Fried Rice

Oven-Roasted Red Potatoes with Rosemary and Garlic

Tomato Grits

Swiss Broccoli Casserole

Sweet Potato Yams

Turnips in Dijon Sauce

Green Rice Casserole

Squash Casserole

Sweet Potato Balls

Mushroom Rice Casserole

Vidalia Onion Casserole

Sweet Stewed Tomatoes

Curry-Crusted Bananas

Mixed Vegetable Casserole

Crunchy New Potatoes

Snow Peas with Grand Marnier

Oven-Fried Potato Wedges

Fried Green Tomatoes with Dijon Pepper Dippin' Sauce

Crème Fraîche Mashed Potatoes

Spicy Tomato Red Rice

Okra Fritters

Sausage-Almond Rice

Crockpot Pinto Beans

Mashed Potato Bake

Cheese Noodles

Italian Potatoes

Noodle Casserole

Corn Chive Pudding

Half-Baked Potato

Cottage Potatoes

Vegetable Pancakes

Hash Brown Potato Casserole

Asparagus Casserole

Pimento Cheese Tomato Bake

Roasted Onions

Green Bean Casserole

Baked Wild Rice

Bo's Eggplant Supreme

Fancy Green Beans

SERVES 6–8

2 tablespoons teriyaki sauce
1 tablespoon honey
1 tablespoon butter
1 tablespoon fresh lemon juice
1½ pounds fresh green beans,
   preferably thin ones, trimmed

2 slices bacon
½ cup red bell pepper, cut into
   strips
½ cup thin onion wedges
½ cup whole cashews

In a small bowl, stir together the teriyaki sauce, honey, and butter. Fill a bowl with cold water and ice cubes. Bring a large pot of water to a boil and add the lemon juice. Drop in the beans and cook for 4 to 5 minutes, or until the beans are bright green. Drain the beans in a colander, then plunge them into ice water; drain again and set aside (this may be done in advance). In a skillet, cook the bacon until very crisp; crumble and set aside. Sauté the bell pepper and onion in the hot bacon fat for 2 minutes. Add the beans, cashews, and bacon to the skillet. Add the teriyaki-honey sauce and toss gently.

Sweet Potato Casserole

SERVES 6–8

1 cup packed brown sugar
1 cup chopped pecans
½ cup self-rising flour
½ cup (1 stick) melted butter
3 cups mashed cooked sweet
   potatoes

1 cup granulated sugar
1 cup coconut flakes
½ cup raisins
2 eggs, lightly beaten
1 teaspoon vanilla extract
¼ cup heavy cream (optional)

For the topping, in a bowl combine the brown sugar, nuts, flour, and ¼ cup of the melted butter, and stir together with a fork; set aside. Mix with a fork. In a large bowl, stir together the sweet potatoes, sugar, coconut, raisins, eggs, and vanilla. If the mixture seems too thick, stir in up to ¼ cup heavy cream. Spoon into a large greased casserole. Spread the topping over the sweet potatoes and bake at 350 degrees for 20 to 30 minutes, or until the topping is golden brown.

❦ ❦ ❦ **The Lady & Sons**

Southern-Style Black-Eyed Peas

SERVES 4–6

1 ham hock, about ½ pound (break it down with a knife, if possible)
2 quarts water
One 16-ounce package frozen black-eyed peas, or fresh black-eyed peas
2 tablespoons butter

½ teaspoon The Lady's House Seasoning
¼ teaspoon The Lady's Seasoned Salt
½ teaspoon Texas Pete Hot Sauce, or 1 small hot pepper (fresh or dried)

Put the ham hock in a stockpot and add the water. Bring to a boil, cover, reduce heat to a simmer, and cook for 1 to 1½ hours. The longer you cook the hock, the stronger your stock will be. When the meat is done you may find that you need to add more water (sometimes I need 2 cups more). Add the peas, butter, House Seasoning, Seasoned Salt, and hot sauce, and return the liquid to a boil. Reduce the heat, cover, and cook over low heat for 20 to 30 minutes, or until the peas are done to your liking. Use this same formula for butter beans, butter peas, crowder peas, or any of their cousins. To make your peas extra special, drop pods of fresh or frozen okra in the pot for the last 10 to 15 minutes of cooking time.

Tomato Casserole

SERVES 6–8

3 tablespoons butter
½ cup chopped onion

½ cup chopped green bell pepper
½ cup chopped celery

One 28-ounce can diced tomatoes
½ cup sugar
2–3 tablespoons chopped fresh basil
Salt and pepper

2 tablespoons cornstarch
2 teaspoons vinegar
2 teaspoons water
1½ cups buttered breadcrumbs

Melt the butter in a large skillet. Add the onion, peppers, and celery, and sauté 3 to 5 minutes, until tender. Add the tomatoes, sugar, basil, and salt and pepper to taste, and bring to a boil. Mix the cornstarch with the vinegar and water, and stir into the skillet. Pour the mixture into a greased casserole and sprinkle with the buttered crumbs. Bake at 350 degrees for 30 to 40 minutes. 🌸 🌸 🌸 **The Lady & Sons**

Saturday Night Vidalia Onions

When I was first married, back in the late sixties and early seventies, going out to eat was reserved for very special occasions. Because of our tight budgets and young children, our social lives consisted of cooking out with our friends on Saturday nights. When the steaks and Vidalia onions were piled on our plates and we took our first bites, I think for a short while we all forgot that we were as poor as church mice, because we were eating like kings. What fond memories these Vidalia onions bring back!

1 large Vidalia onion, or a comparable sweet onion, per person
1 tablespoon butter per onion

1 beef bouillon cube per onion
Pepper

Prepare a fire in a charcoal grill. Trim a slice from the top of each onion, and peel the onion without cutting off the root end. With a potato peeler, cut a small cone-shaped section from the center of the onion. Cut the onion into quarters from the top down, stopping within a half inch of the root end. Place a bouillon cube in the center, slip slivers of butter in between the sections, and sprinkle with pepper. Wrap each onion in a double thickness of heavy-duty foil. Place the onions directly onto the hot coals and cook for 45 minutes, turning every so often. These can also be baked in a 350-degree oven for 45 minutes, but I still say they're better grilled over charcoal. Serve in individual bowls because they produce a lot of broth, which tastes like French onion soup.

Corn Casserole

SERVES 6–8

One 15¼-ounce can whole kernel
  corn, drained
One 14¾-ounce can cream-style
  corn

One 8-ounce package Jiffy corn
  muffin mix
1 cup sour cream
½ cup (1 stick) melted butter

In a large bowl, stir together the two cans of corn, corn muffin mix, sour cream, and butter. Pour into a greased casserole. Bake at 350 degrees for 45 to 60 minutes, or until golden brown.

🌣 🌣 🌣 **The Lady & Sons**

Jelly Roll's Crab Fried Rice

SERVES 6–8

This dish is delicious served alongside a nice fresh fish or stuffed inside a fish fillet.

½ cup (1 stick) butter
1 medium onion, diced
1 medium green bell pepper, diced
1 pound claw crabmeat, picked
  free of any broken shells
2 cups cooked white rice

1 teaspoon The Lady's House
  Seasoning
1 teaspoon Accent (optional)
¼ cup chopped fresh parsley

Melt the butter in a large skillet. Add the onions and green pepper and sauté until tender, about 5 minutes. Add the crabmeat, rice, House Seasoning, and Accent, and mix well. Stir in the parsley and simmer over low heat for 15 minutes.

🌣 🌣 🌣 **The Lady & Sons**

Oven-Roasted Red Potatoes with Rosemary and Garlic

SERVES 6

1½ pounds small new red potatoes (about 15), scrubbed and dried
¼ cup extra-virgin olive oil

4–6 cloves garlic, crushed
1 tablespoon fresh or 1 teaspoon dried rosemary

Pare a narrow strip of peel from the middle of each potato. In a large bowl mix the oil, garlic, and rosemary; add the potatoes and toss well. Transfer the potatoes to a shallow baking pan and roast at 350 degrees until the potatoes are tender when tested with the tip of a knife. Serve hot. These can also be chilled and served with fried chicken or ham.

Tomato Grits

SERVES 8–10

2 cups water
1¼ cups milk
1 teaspoon salt
1 cup quick-cooking grits
½ cup (1 stick), plus 1 tablespoon butter
⅓ cup diced green onions

One 6-ounce Kraft Garlic Cheese Roll
2½ cups shredded Cheddar cheese
One 10-ounce can Ro-Tel diced tomatoes and green chilies
2 eggs, lightly beaten

Preheat the oven to 350 degrees. In a saucepan, bring the water and milk to a boil. Add the salt. Slowly add the grits and return to a boil; stir for 1 full minute. (The secret to preparing good grits is the initial stirring of the pot.) Reduce the heat, cover, and cook for 3 minutes. Stir the grits and add 1 stick of butter, stirring until it has melted. Cover and cook for 3 to 5 minutes, or until the grits are thick and creamy. Remove from the heat and set aside. Sauté the onions in the remaining 1 tablespoon butter for 1 minute. Add the garlic cheese, 1½ cups Cheddar, and onions to the grits, and stir until the cheese is melted. Add the tomatoes and mix well; stir in the beaten eggs. Pour the grits into a greased 8 × 11 × 2-inch casserole. Bake the casserole for 40 minutes. Sprinkle the remaining cheese over the casserole for the last 5 minutes of cooking time.   ❦ ❦ ❦   **The Lady & Sons**

Swiss Broccoli Casserole

SERVES 6

*Two 10-ounce packages frozen
    broccoli spears, cooked and
    drained*
3 hard-boiled eggs, sliced
2 cups french-fried onion rings

½ cup shredded Swiss cheese
*One 10¾-ounce can of cream of
    celery soup*
⅔ cup milk

Preheat the oven to 350 degrees. Arrange the broccoli in a shallow 2-quart baking dish. Layer the eggs, 1 cup of the onion rings, and then the cheese over the broccoli. Combine the soup and milk, mixing well. Pour this over the cheese and bake for 25 minutes. Top with the remaining onion rings and bake for 5 minutes longer.

Sweet Potato Yams

SERVES 4

3 large sweet potatoes
3 cups water
1½ cups sugar
1 teaspoon vanilla extract

4 tablespoons butter
½–1 teaspoon cinnamon
¼ teaspoon freshly grated nutmeg

Wash and dry the sweet potatoes. Bake at 400 degrees for 1 hour, or until the potatoes are soft to the touch. Remove from the oven and let cool slightly. Reduce the oven heat to 350 degrees. While the potatoes are baking, combine the remaining ingredients in a saucepan; bring to a boil, then reduce the heat and simmer for 30 minutes, or until the sauce is slightly thickened. Slice the potatoes ½ inch thick into a medium casserole, pour the sauce over them, and return to the oven for 15 minutes, or until hot. ❧ ❧ ❧ *The Lady & Sons*

Turnips in Dijon Sauce

SERVES 4–6

2 medium turnips, peeled and
   sliced
1 medium potato, peeled and
   diced
1 carrot, diced
1 onion, diced

1 stalk celery, diced
½ cup mayonnaise
1 tablespoon Dijon mustard
1 tablespoon fresh lemon juice
Freshly ground pepper

Steam the vegetables for 10 minutes, or until tender. Combine the mayonnaise, mustard, lemon juice, and pepper in a small saucepan and heat gently. Add the vegetables to the sauce and stir to coat the vegetables. Serve immediately.

Green Rice Casserole

SERVES 6–8

One 10-ounce package frozen
   chopped broccoli
2 cups cooked rice
One 10¾-ounce can cream of
   mushroom soup

½ cup (1 stick) butter, at room
   temperature
One 8-ounce jar Cheez-Wiz

Cook the broccoli according to package directions; drain well. In a large bowl, combine the broccoli, rice, soup, and butter. Reserving a small amount for the top of the casserole, add the Cheez-Wiz. Stir until the butter and Cheez-Wiz are blended in. Transfer to a greased casserole and top with remaining Cheez-Wiz. Bake at 325 degrees for 30 minutes, or until the top starts to bubble.

❧ ❧ ❧ *The Lady & Sons*

Squash Casserole

SERVES 4

2 cups cooked mashed yellow squash
2 cups Ritz Cracker crumbs
1 cup evaporated milk
1 cup shredded cheese, such as
   Cheddar or Swiss
1 cup chopped onion

2 eggs, lightly beaten
1 teaspoon salt
1 teaspoon pepper
Pinch of sugar
6 tablespoons butter

Place the squash in a large bowl. Add the cracker crumbs, milk, cheese, and onion, and stir well. Stir in the eggs, salt, pepper, sugar, and butter, and pour into a greased 1-quart casserole. Bake at 350 degrees for 40 minutes.   ❧ ❧ ❧   *The Lady & Sons*

Sweet Potato Balls

SERVES 4–6

4 large sweet potatoes
⅔ cup packed brown sugar
2 tablespoons orange juice
1 teaspoon orange zest
½ teaspoon freshly grated nutmeg

2 cups shredded coconut
½ cup granulated sugar
1 teaspoon cinnamon
8 large marshmallows

Bake the potatoes until tender, then peel and mash them (the potatoes can be baked the day before). Stir in the sugar, orange juice, zest, and nutmeg. Toss the coconut with the sugar and cinnamon. Press mashed potatoes around each marshmallow, then roll the balls in the coconut mixture. Bake at 350 degrees for 15 to 20 minutes. Watch carefully for the last few minutes of cooking; the expanding marshmallows can cause the potato balls to burst open. These are wonderful served with turkey or ham.

Sugar-and-Nut-Glazed Brie

Zesty Cheese Straws

Chef Jack's Corn Chowder

BLT Soup

Taco Soup

The Best Crab Casserole

Hurry-Up Chicken Pot Pie

Chicken Boudine

Out shopping for veggies

Sweet Potato Balls

Sweet Potato Biscuits

Gorilla Bread

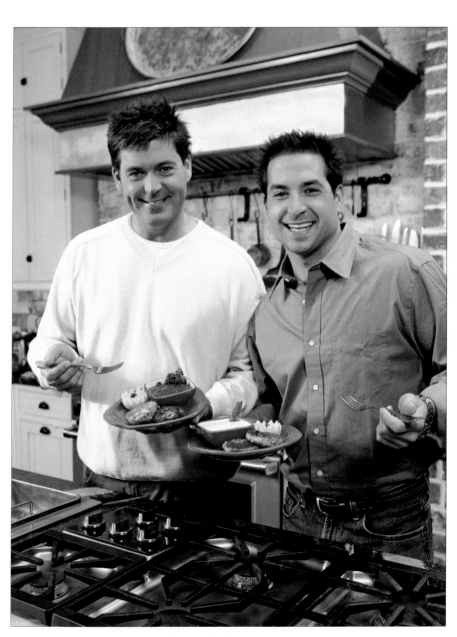

Crab Cakes with Lemon Dill Sauce
(left to right: Jamie Deen and Bobby Deen)

Lucile Wright's Tomato Sandwiches

Pumpkin Gingerbread Trifle

Grandgirl's Fresh Apple Cake from Georgia

Mushroom Rice Casserole

SERVES 4–6

5 tablespoons butter
1 cup sliced fresh mushrooms
1 cup chopped onion
1 cup raw long-grain rice

One 10 ¾-ounce can cream of
  mushroom soup
One 10 ¾-ounce can beef consommé

Heat the butter in a skillet. Sauté the mushrooms and onions for 3 to 5 minutes, then stir in the rice and sauté for 3 minutes longer, stirring constantly. Stir in the soup and consommé. Pour the mixture into a greased casserole, cover, and bake at 350 degrees for 45 to 60 minutes. Check the rice after 30 minutes; if it is drying out, add a little boiling water. ❧ ❧ ❧ **The Lady & Sons**

Vidalia Onion Casserole

SERVES 4–6

4 large Vidalia onions, quartered
7 tablespoons butter
3 eggs
One 5-ounce can evaporated milk

1 tube Ritz Crackers, crushed
1½ cups grated Cheddar cheese
Salt and pepper

Boil the onions until tender; drain. Heat 4 tablespoons of the butter in a skillet and sauté the onions. Beat the eggs and milk together. Add the onions, half the cracker crumbs, the cheese, and salt and pepper to taste. Bake in a buttered casserole at 375 degrees for 35 minutes. Melt the remaining 3 tablespoons butter and stir it into the remaining cracker crumbs. Top the casserole with the buttered crumbs and bake for 15 minutes longer. ❧ ❧ ❧ **The Lady & Sons**

Sweet Stewed Tomatoes

SERVES 6

During the winter months I recommend using canned tomatoes, but in the summer, don't miss the chance to use vine-ripened fresh tomatoes.

5 large fresh tomatoes, or 4 cups
  canned diced tomatoes
4 tablespoons bacon drippings or
  butter
1 cup diced onions
2 cloves garlic, minced
1 teaspoon The Lady's House
  Seasoning

3 tablespoons sugar
2 tablespoons chopped fresh parsley
1 tablespoon cornstarch
3 tablespoons milk
¼ cup grated Parmesan (optional)

If using fresh tomatoes, peel and dice them. Heat the drippings in a skillet and sauté the onions and garlic, stirring to prevent the garlic from burning. Add the House Seasoning and tomatoes, cover the pan, and cook over medium-low heat for 35 minutes. Add the sugar and parsley. Mix the cornstarch and milk until smooth. Bring the tomatoes to a boil and pour in the cornstarch mixture, stirring constantly. Add the Parmesan, if using, and stir well. The stewed tomatoes are wonderful served over rice.   ❧ ❧ ❧   **The Lady & Sons**

Curry-Crusted Bananas

SERVES 8

These bananas—crispy on the outside and soft on the inside—are wonderful served with baked ham, pork chops, or lamb.

4 firm bananas, peeled
6 tablespoons melted butter
1 teaspoon curry powder

2 cups crushed cornflakes
Sugar for sprinkling (optional)

Preheat the oven to 450 degrees. Halve the bananas lengthwise, then crosswise. In a bowl, mix the butter and curry powder. Dip the bananas in butter, coating well. Roll the bananas in the cornflakes until completely coated and sprinkle with sugar, if desired. Place the bananas in a greased baking dish and bake for 10 minutes. ❧ ❧ ❧ **The Lady & Sons**

Mixed Vegetable Casserole

SERVES 6

One 15-ounce can Veg-All,
   drained
One 8-ounce can sliced water
   chestnuts, drained
1 cup grated sharp cheese

1 cup chopped celery
¾ cup mayonnaise
1 small onion, chopped
20 Ritz Crackers, crushed
2 tablespoons melted butter

In a large bowl, mix the Veg-All, water chestnuts, cheese, celery, mayonnaise, and onion; transfer to a greased casserole. Bake at 350 degrees for 30 minutes.

Meanwhile, combine the cracker crumbs and butter. When the casserole has baked for 30 minutes, sprinkle it with the buttered crumbs and return it to the oven to brown. ❧ ❧ ❧ **The Lady & Sons**

Crunchy New Potatoes

SERVES 4

12 small new red potatoes
One 0.4-ounce package Hidden
   Valley Original Ranch
   Buttermilk Recipe mix

2 cups crushed cornflakes
½ cup (1 stick) melted butter

Cook the potatoes in boiling water until tender, 20 to 25 minutes. Preheat the oven to 400 degrees. Drain the potatoes and let cool slightly, then peel them. Mix dressing mix and the cornflakes in a bowl. Dip the potatoes in melted butter, then roll them in the cornflake mixture. Place the potatoes in a greased baking dish and bake for 20 to 25 minutes, or until golden brown. ❧ ❧ ❧ **The Lady & Sons**

Snow Peas with Grand Marnier

SERVES 8

1 cup water
1 teaspoon sugar
Three 10-ounce packages frozen
   snow peas
One 8-ounce can sliced water
   chestnuts, drained

¼ cup Grand Marnier
5 tablespoons butter
1 tablespoon chopped fresh mint, or
   1½ tablespoons dried mint
1 teaspoon salt

Bring 1 cup of water to a boil and add the sugar. Drop in the snow peas and cook until barely tender, drain, and return to pan. Add the water chestnuts, Grand Marnier, butter, mint, and salt. Cook over medium-low heat until heated through.

Oven-Fried Potato Wedges

SERVES 6

3 large baking potatoes
½ cup mayonnaise
½ teaspoon Texas Pete Hot Sauce
¼ teaspoon onion salt

¼ teaspoon The Lady's Seasoned Salt
⅛ teaspoon black pepper
2 cups Pepperidge Farm
   Cornbread Dressing Mix

Preheat the oven to 375 degrees. Wash the potatoes and cut into thick wedges (each potato should yield six wedges). Mix the mayonnaise with the hot sauce, onion salt, Seasoned Salt, and pepper. Coat the potato wedges with the mayonnaise mixture and roll them in the dressing mix. Place in a greased baking dish and bake for 45 to 50 minutes, or until the potatoes are tender. Goes great with a good ol' char-grilled hamburger.

Fried Green Tomatoes with Dijon Pepper Dippin' Sauce

SERVES 6

This recipe is a new twist on one in The Lady & Sons Savannah Country Cookbook. *Dip into the Dijon sauce with care—it's a little on the hot side. We like to put a small dollop of roasted red pepper vinaigrette on each tomato slice.*

3 or 4 large firm green tomatoes	1 cup buttermilk
Salt	2 cups self-rising flour
2 cups vegetable or peanut oil for deep-frying	Dijon Pepper Dippin' Sauce (recipe follows)

Slice the tomatoes ¼ inch thick. Lay them out in a shallow baking pan and sprinkle with salt. Place the tomato slices in a colander and allow time for the salt to pull the water out of the tomatoes (30 minutes should do it).

In a skillet heat the oil for deep-frying over medium-high heat.

Dip the tomatoes into buttermilk, then dredge them in flour. Deep-fry until golden brown. ❦ ❦ ❦ **The Lady & Sons**

DIJON PEPPER DIPPIN' SAUCE

MAKES 2 CUPS

1 cup Dijon mustard	½ cup vegetable oil
½ cup mayonnaise	1 tablespoon red pepper flakes
2 tablespoons balsamic vinegar	1 tablespoon whole peppercorns
1 tablespoon white pepper	
4 tablespoons coarsely ground black pepper	

In the bowl of a food processor, combine the mustard, mayonnaise, balsamic vinegar, white pepper, and 1 tablespoon of the black pepper, and beat until just blended; set aside.

In a small saucepan combine the oil, the remaining 3 tablespoons of black pepper, the red pepper flakes, and the whole peppercorns. Heat the oil until hot, then reduce the heat to low and simmer for 20 minutes. Allow to cool, then strain. With the food processor running, drizzle the oil into the mayonnaise mixture. Continue processing for 2 minutes.

🌿 🌿 🌿 *The Lady & Sons*

Crème Fraîche Mashed Potatoes

SERVES 8

1 cup, plus 2 tablespoons heavy cream

¾ cup sour cream

2 pounds small red potatoes

1 teaspoon salt

One 8-ounce package cream cheese, at room temperature

2 teaspoons roasted garlic (from a jar, or homemade)

1 teaspoon The Lady's House Seasoning

1 teaspoon The Lady's Seasoned Salt

4 tablespoons butter, slivered

¼ cup sliced green onions

1 tablespoon chopped fresh chives

Prepare the crème fraîche ahead of time by combining 1 cup of the heavy cream with ½ cup of the sour cream. Cover with plastic wrap and let stand at room temperature for 12 to 24 hours, or until thick. Stir well and refrigerate for at least 4 hours. Crème fraîche will keep for up to 2 weeks.

Put the potatoes in a pot and cover with cold water. Add the salt and bring to a boil. Cook until the potatoes are tender, 20 to 25 minutes; drain. Preheat the oven to 350 degrees. With an electric mixer, beat the potatoes with the cream cheese, the remaining ¼ cup sour cream, and the 2 tablespoons of heavy cream, the garlic, House Seasoning, and Seasoned Salt. Stir in the butter and onions. Place the mashed potatoes in a lightly greased 2-quart round casserole. Spoon the crème fraîche on top and sprinkle with chives. Bake until the potatoes are hot, 20 to 30 minutes.

🌿 🌿 🌿 *The Lady & Sons*

Spicy Tomato Red Rice

SERVES 4

4 strips bacon
1 medium onion
1 small green bell pepper
1 cup raw rice
One 14½-ounce can whole
   tomatoes, with liquid

1 cup water
One 6-ounce can tomato paste
1 teaspoon sugar
1 teaspoon salt
1 teaspoon hot sauce

Fry the bacon in a heavy saucepan; remove the bacon from the pan and set aside. Sauté the onion and bell pepper in the bacon fat. Add the rice and stir until it is coated with fat; crumble in the bacon. Add the tomatoes, water, tomato paste, sugar, salt, and hot sauce, and bring to a boil. Cook covered over low heat for 20 minutes. Remove from the heat and let stand for 20 minutes longer. *Do not peek!*

❦ ❦ ❦   **The Lady & Sons**

Okra Fritters

SERVES 4–6

1½ cups all-purpose flour
1 tablespoon The Lady's House
   Seasoning
⅓ cup buttermilk

4 cups cut okra, fresh or frozen
   (thawed if frozen)
6 cups vegetable oil (for deep-
   frying)

Mix the flour and House Seasoning. Pour the buttermilk over the okra and toss to coat. Place the okra in the flour mixture and toss; shake off any excess flour. Heat the oil in a cast-iron Dutch oven. When it registers 350 degrees, add the okra and fry until golden brown, 13 to 15 minutes.

❦ ❦ ❦   **The Lady & Sons**

Sausage-Almond Rice

SERVES 6

3 cups water
One 2.1-ounce package chicken
    noodle soup
1 pound ground pork sausage
1 cup raw rice

1 cup chopped celery
½ cup chopped onion
½ cup chopped green bell pepper
¼ cup sliced almonds

Preheat the oven to 350 degrees. Combine the water and soup mix in a saucepan and simmer for 10 minutes. Meanwhile, brown the sausage and rice in a large skillet. Add the celery, onions, and bell pepper, and mix well. Combine the rice mixture with the soup, add the almonds, and pour into a greased casserole; cover and bake for 1 hour.

Crockpot Pinto Beans

SERVES 8

1 pound dry pinto beans
¼ pound streak o' lean, or
    ½ pound ham hocks*
4 cups water

1 onion, chopped
1 teaspoon chili powder
½ teaspoon dried oregano
The Lady's House Seasoning

Wash the beans and place in a large pot. Add enough cold water to cover and soak overnight.

Drain the beans. If using streak o' lean, cut it into cubes, brown in a skillet, and place the meat and any rendered fat in the crockpot. Add the water, onion, chili powder, and oregano. Add the drained beans and stir well.

Season to taste with House Seasoning, cover the pot, and cook on high for 5 hours.

*If using ham hocks, try to break them down some, using a sharp knife.

Mashed Potato Bake

SERVES 8

5 cups water
4 cups frozen hash brown potatoes
One 7.6-ounce package Betty
   Crocker Butter and Herb
   Mashed Potatoes mix
½ cup (1 stick) butter
4 ounces cream cheese

1 cup Monterey Jack cheese
½ cup sour cream
½ teaspoon garlic salt
½ teaspoon salt
½ teaspoon pepper
2 cups canned french-fried onion
   rings

Preheat the oven to 350 degrees. Bring the water to a boil, add the hash browns, and cook for 5 minutes; drain. Prepare the mashed-potato mix according to package directions. Soften the butter and cream cheese together in the microwave. In a large bowl, mix together the hash browns, mashed potatoes, butter and cream cheese, Jack cheese, sour cream, garlic salt, salt, and pepper. Place in a greased 2-quart casserole. Bake for 25 to 35 minutes, or until golden on top. Sprinkle the onion rings over the casserole and bake for about 5 to 8 minutes longer, or until onions are golden brown.   🐾 🐾 🐾 **The Lady & Sons**

Cheese Noodles

SERVES 6–8

1 cup cottage cheese
1 cup sour cream
One 6-ounce package fine-cut
   noodles, cooked and drained

2 tablespoons grated onion
1 teaspoon Worcestershire sauce
½–¾ teaspoon garlic salt
½ cup grated Parmesan

Stir together the cottage cheese and sour cream, and add this to the noodles. Add the onion, Worcestershire sauce, and garlic salt to taste, and place in a greased casserole. Sprinkle the Parmesan over the casserole and bake at 350 degrees for 45 minutes.

🐾 🐾 🐾 **The Lady & Sons**

Italian Potatoes

SERVES 16

14 or 15 large red potatoes (about 5 pounds)
½ cup chopped fresh parsley
½ cup chopped green onions
3 large cloves garlic, thinly sliced
1 heaping teaspoon salt
½ teaspoon dry mustard
1 scant tablespoon sugar
1 tablespoon Worcestershire sauce
1 cup olive oil
½ cup tarragon vinegar

Boil the potatoes until tender. When done peel and cut in 1-inch chunks. Sprinkle parsley and green onions over the potatoes. Make the sauce by mixing the rest of the ingredients; then pour over the potatoes. Stir well. Let it stand all day (or at least 4 hours). Stir every hour. Do not refrigerate. ❦ ❦ ❦ *The Lady & Sons*

Noodle Casserole

SERVES 4

¼ cup (½ stick) butter
One 8-ounce can sliced mushrooms, drained, or 1 cup sliced fresh mushrooms
¼ cup finely chopped onion
¼ cup finely sliced blanched almonds
1 clove garlic, minced, or ¼ teaspoon garlic purée
1 tablespoon fresh lemon juice
One 10¾-ounce can French onion soup
2 cups fine-cut noodles, uncooked

Melt the butter in a large skillet. Add the mushrooms, onions, almonds, garlic, and lemon juice, and sauté gently for about 10 minutes. Stir in the soup and bring to a boil. Add the noodles; reduce the heat, cover, and simmer for about 5 minutes. This is very good served with chicken or beef. ❦ ❦ ❦ *The Lady & Sons*

Corn Chive Pudding

SERVES 8

*Two 10-ounce packages frozen
corn, thawed*
¼ cup sugar
1¼ teaspoons salt
4 large eggs
2 cups milk

*¼ cup (½ stick) melted unsalted
butter, cooled*
¼ cup chopped fresh chives
3 tablespoons all-purpose flour
1 teaspoon vanilla extract
Pinch of freshly grated nutmeg

Preheat the oven to 350 degrees. Butter a 1½-quart baking dish. In a
food processor, pulse half of the corn until coarsely chopped; transfer
to a mixing bowl. Add the remaining corn and sprinkle with the sugar
and salt; stir to combine. Whisk together the eggs, milk, butter, chives,
flour, and vanilla, and combine with the corn. Pour into the baking
dish and sprinkle with nutmeg. Bake in the center of the oven until the
center of the pudding is just set, about 45 minutes.

Half-Baked Potato

SERVES 1

This recipe is for one person—you can expand it as necessary.

1 large baking potato
*2 tablespoons olive oil or melted
butter*

¼ cup grated Parmesan
¼ teaspoon paprika

Cut the potato in half lengthwise. Brush the cut sides with olive oil or
butter. Mix Parmesan and paprika together. Dip the cut sides in the
Parmesan and paprika mix. Place the potato, cut sides down, on a
greased pan, and bake at 350 degrees for 1 hour.

🍀 🍀 🍀 **The Lady & Sons**

Cottage Potatoes

SERVES 4

3 large Idaho potatoes
¼ cup (½ stick) butter
1 cup cottage cheese

½ onion, diced
Salt and pepper
Paprika

Scrub the potatoes, slice them, and put in a pot with water to cover. Boil the potatoes until tender, then drain and mash them with 2 table-spoons of the butter. Add the cottage cheese, onion, and salt and pepper to taste. Stir the mixture gently, then put it in a greased casserole. Dot with the remaining 2 tablespoons of butter and sprinkle with paprika. Bake, uncovered, at 350 degrees for 30 minutes.

❦ ❦ ❦   **The Lady & Sons**

Vegetable Pancakes

SERVES 8

These pancakes are delicious with a dollop of sour cream.

½ cup all-purpose flour
½ teaspoon baking powder
½ teaspoon salt
¼ teaspoon pepper
1 egg
¼ cup milk

1 cup grated carrots (about 2
  carrots)
1 cup grated zucchini (1 medium
  zucchini)
2 green onions, sliced
2 tablespoons vegetable oil

In a mixing bowl, stir together the flour, baking powder, salt, and pepper. In another bowl, beat together the egg, milk, carrots, zucchini, and onions. Add this to the dry ingredients and stir until just combined. Heat 1 tablespoon of the oil in a large skillet over medium heat. Pour the batter by tablespoonfuls into the pan, making a few pancakes at a time. Cook until golden, about 2 minutes on each side. Add the remaining oil to the pan as needed. Serve at once.

Hash Brown Potato Casserole

SERVES 10–12

*2 pounds frozen hash brown
  potatoes
4 cups grated Cheddar cheese
One 10¾-ounce can cream of
  chicken or cream of mushroom
  soup*

*2 cups sour cream
½ cup (1 stick) melted butter
1 medium onion, chopped
2 teaspoons The Lady's House
  Seasoning*

Preheat the oven to 350 degrees. In a large bowl, combine the potatoes, 2 cups of the Cheddar, the soup, sour cream, butter, onion, and House Seasoning. Place in a buttered 13 × 9 × 2-inch pan and bake for 35 minutes. Remove from the oven and top with the remaining Cheddar. Return to the oven and bake for 10 minutes longer.

VARIATION: Instead of topping the casserole with cheese, you may use 2 cups crushed Ritz Crackers mixed with a ½ cup melted butter.

❧ ❧ ❧   *The Lady & Sons*

Asparagus Casserole

SERVES 6

*2 tablespoons butter
2 tablespoons all-purpose flour
2 cups milk
Two 15-ounce cans asparagus
  spears, drained*

*1 cup grated Cheddar cheese
4 hard-boiled eggs, sliced
Salt and pepper
1 cup breadcrumbs*

To make the sauce, heat the butter in a skillet; stir in the flour, mixing well, then add the milk all at once. Cook over medium heat, stirring constantly, until thick and creamy; set aside. Arrange half of the asparagus in the bottom of a buttered 2-quart casserole. Top with half of the Cheddar and half of the egg slices. Sprinkle with salt and pepper to taste. Pour half of the sauce on top. Repeat the layers beginning with the remaining asparagus. Top with the breadcrumbs and bake at 350 degrees for 30 minutes. ❦ ❦ ❦ *The Lady & Sons*

Pimento Cheese Tomato Bake

SERVES 8–10

1 cup grated sharp Cheddar cheese
1 cup grated Monterey Jack cheese
½ cup mayonnaise
One 3-ounce package cream cheese, at room temperature
3 tablespoons mashed pimentos
½ teaspoon The Lady's House Seasoning, plus more to taste
1 teaspoon grated onion

Cracked pepper
12 slices white bread, trimmed of crusts
2 or 3 ripe tomatoes, sliced
2 teaspoons chopped fresh oregano, or 1 teaspoon dried oregano
One 10-ounce can Ro-Tel diced tomatoes with green chilies

Preheat the oven to 350 degrees. Using an electric mixer, beat together the Cheddar and Jack cheeses, the mayonnaise, cream cheese, pimentos, House Seasoning, onion, and cracked pepper to taste. Spread the pimento cheese mixture on one side of each slice of bread. Roll each slice up jelly-roll style. Place the fresh tomato slices in an 8 × 11 × 2-inch baking dish, covering the entire bottom. Sprinkle the tomatoes with half of the oregano and House Seasoning to taste. Place the rolls on top of the sliced tomatoes, pour the canned tomatoes evenly over them, and sprinkle with the remaining oregano. Bake for 30 minutes. ❦ ❦ ❦ *The Lady & Sons*

Roasted Onions

SERVES 4–6

2 or 3 large Vidalia onions
½ cup chopped fresh mint
3 tablespoons extra-virgin olive oil
2 tablespoons chopped garlic

1 teaspoon salt, or to taste
½ teaspoon freshly ground black pepper, or to taste
¼ cup balsamic vinegar

Peel and trim the onions. Cut each one in half through the stem and root end. In a medium bowl, stir together the mint, oil, garlic, salt, and pepper. With your hands, coat the onions with this mixture and place the onions in a roasting pan. Bake at 350 degrees for 30 minutes. Baste the onions with the juices and continue roasting for 15 minutes longer, or until the onions are soft when pierced with a knife. Remove the pan from the oven and drizzle the vinegar over the onions. Arrange the onions on a platter.   ❦ ❦ ❦   *The Lady & Sons*

Green Bean Casserole

SERVES 6

3 tablespoons butter
½ cup diced onions
½ cup sliced fresh mushrooms
2 cups cooked sliced green beans, drained
One 10 ¾-ounce can cream of mushroom soup

One 2.8-ounce can french-fried onion rings
The Lady's House Seasoning
1 cup grated Cheddar cheese

Preheat the oven to 350 degrees. Melt the butter in a large skillet. Sauté the onions and mushrooms in the butter. Add the green beans, mushroom soup, onion rings, and House Seasoning to taste. Stir well. Pour into a greased 1½-quart baking dish. Bake for 20 minutes, then top the casserole with the Cheddar and bake for 10 minutes longer, or until the casserole is hot and cheese is melted.

❦ ❦ ❦   *The Lady & Sons*

Baked Wild Rice

SERVES 6

½ pound raw wild rice
1 cup (2 sticks) butter
1 pound fresh mushrooms
1 medium white onion, chopped

2 teaspoons all-purpose flour
1 cup heavy cream
½ cup sherry
½ cup buttered breadcrumbs

Cook the rice according to package directions. Drain and return the pot to the heat briefly to steam the rice dry. Melt the butter in a large skillet. Sauté the mushrooms and onion, then push them to one side of the pan and add the flour. Stir until the mushrooms are coated with butter. Add the cream, stirring constantly. Add the sherry and stir until smooth. Fold in the cooked rice. Pour into a greased casserole and top with breadcrumbs. Bake at 350 degrees for about 30 minutes, or until the top is brown.

Bo's Eggplant Supreme

SERVES 4–6

1 large eggplant
1 teaspoon The Lady's House
  Seasoning
5 tablespoons butter

One 10-ounce can minced clams,
  drained, juice reserved
1 cup cracker crumbs
½ cup half-and-half

Peel the eggplant and cut it into thin rounds. Bring a pot of water to boil. Add the House Seasoning, then the eggplant, and cook for 10 to 15 minutes, or until tender. Drain the eggplant well and mash it with 2 tablespoons of the butter. In a greased casserole, layer the mashed eggplant, the clams, and the cracker crumbs. Dot with the remaining 3 tablespoons of butter. Blend the half-and-half with the reserved clam juice. Taste, and add salt, if needed. Pour this mixture over the casserole and bake at 350 degrees for 30 minutes.

Breads

Plantation Skillet Cake

Currant and Oat Scones

Popovers

Cheese Muffins

Easy Yeast Rolls

Crunchy Peanut Butter Muffins

The Lady & Sons Onion-Cheese Bread

Riz Biscuits

Blackberry Muffins

Easy Herb Rolls

Pineapple Upside-Down Biscuits

Green Muffins

Sour Cream Butter Biscuits

Old-Time Spoon Bread

Sweet Potato Biscuits

Hush Puppies

Apple Raisin Muffins

Gorilla Bread

Nutty Orange Coffee Cake

Cheesy French Bread

Corny Corn Muffins

Banana Bread

Plantation Skillet Cake

SERVES 4–6

This is a delicious breakfast dish, very easily prepared and quick to cook. It is something like Yorkshire pudding.

3 eggs
½ cup all-purpose flour
¼ teaspoon salt

½ cup milk
2 tablespoons vegetable oil

Preheat the oven to 400 degrees. Beat the eggs well, then add the flour and salt and beat again. Slowly add the milk, then the oil, beating constantly. Butter an 8-inch cast-iron skillet generously and pour in the batter. Bake for about 20 minutes, or until the cake is puffed and brown at the edges. Cut the cake in wedges and serve it with warm applesauce and brown sugar.

Currant and Oat Scones

YIELDS 12 SCONES

1½ cups all-purpose flour
1¼ cups rolled oats
¼ cup, plus 1 teaspoon sugar
1 tablespoon baking powder
¼ teaspoon salt

⅓ cup margarine
1 cup dried currants
½ cup milk
1 egg, lightly beaten
⅛ teaspoon cinnamon

Preheat the oven to 375 degrees. In a mixing bowl, combine the flour, oats, ¼ cup of the sugar, the baking powder, and salt. Cut in the margarine until the mixture resembles course crumbs. Stir in the currants. In a small bowl, combine the milk and egg. Add the milk mixture to the flour mixture and stir until just moistened. Shape the dough into a ball. Working on a lightly floured surface, knead the dough gently 6 times. On a lightly greased baking sheet, pat out the dough to form an

8-inch circle. Using a sharp knife, score the round into 12 wedges. Stir together the remaining 1 teaspoon sugar and the cinnamon. Sprinkle this over the dough and bake for 20 to 25 minutes, or until golden brown. Break apart the wedges. Serve warm.

Popovers

YIELDS 12 POPOVERS

These popovers are so good it's hard to believe they are so simple to make. The secret is starting with a cold oven. And don't peek for the full 30 minutes.

4 eggs
2 cups milk

2 cups all-purpose flour
1 teaspoon salt

Grease 12 large muffin-tin cups or 12 custard cups. If using custard cups, place them in a shallow pan. Break the eggs into a bowl; beat well with a fork or whisk. Add the milk, flour, and salt, and beat until just blended. Fill the muffin tins or custard cups three-quarters full with the batter. Place the pan on a rack in the center of the oven. Set the oven at 450 degrees and turn it on. Bake for 30 minutes without opening the oven door. Serve the popovers hot with plenty of butter, jam, syrup, or honey.

Cheese Muffins

YIELDS ABOUT 12 MUFFINS

These delectable muffins are so rich they can be served with nothing more than a large green salad for a luncheon.

1½ cups all-purpose flour
1 tablespoon sugar
2½ teaspoons baking powder
½ teaspoon salt
3 cups coarsely grated Cheddar
cheese

1 egg
1 cup milk
¼ cup (½ stick) melted butter

Preheat the oven to 350 degrees. Sift together the flour, sugar, baking powder, and salt. Stir the Cheddar into the dry ingredients until all the particles of cheese are coated with flour. Beat the egg with the milk and stir this into the flour mixture until just blended, then add the butter. Bake the batter in greased muffin tins for 20 minutes.

Easy Yeast Rolls

YIELDS 15 ROLLS

One ¼-ounce package dry yeast
¾ cup warm water (105–115 degrees)
2½ cups, plus ½–1 cup The Lady & Sons Biscuit Mix, or any prepared biscuit mix

1 teaspoon sugar
¼ cup (½ stick) melted butter

Preheat the oven to 400 degrees. Dissolve the yeast in the water. Put the 2½ cups of Biscuit Mix in a large bowl; stir in the sugar. Add the yeast mixture, stirring vigorously. Sprinkle the work surface generously with the remaining ½–1 cup Biscuit Mix. Turn the dough out onto the surface and knead well 15 to 20 times. Shape the dough as desired. (I shape heaping tablespoons of dough into balls.) Place on a lightly greased baking sheet, cover with a damp cloth, and let rise in a warm place for 1 hour. Bake for 12 to 15 minutes, or until golden brown. Brush the rolls with melted butter while they're hot.

Crunchy Peanut Butter Muffins

YIELDS 15 MUFFINS

MUFFINS
2 cups all-purpose flour
4 teaspoons baking powder
2 teaspoons cinnamon
¾ teaspoon salt
¼ cup peanut butter (crunchy or
    smooth)
¼ cup peanut oil
¾ cup packed light brown sugar
1 very ripe banana, mashed

¾ cup milk
1 egg

TOPPING
½ teaspoon cinnamon
¼ cup packed light brown sugar
2 tablespoons butter
1 cup unsalted roasted peanuts,
    chopped

Preheat the oven to 400 degrees. For the muffins, stir the flour with the baking powder, cinnamon, and salt until well blended; set aside. In a separate bowl, beat the peanut butter with the peanut oil, sugar, and banana. Add in the milk and egg and beat until smooth. Pour this mixture into the center of the dry ingredients and stir with a large spoon until just moistened. Line 2½-inch muffin tins with paper or foil liners and fill the cups two-thirds full with batter.

For the topping, stir the cinnamon into the sugar. Using a pastry blender or two knives, cut the butter into the sugar until the mixture is crumbly. Lightly stir in the peanuts; set aside. Sprinkle the topping evenly over each batter-filled cup.

Bake for 18 to 20 minutes, or until the muffins spring back if lightly pressed in their centers.

The Lady & Sons Onion-Cheese Bread

YIELDS 8 WEDGES

This bread is wonderful served along with our Baked Spaghetti (see page 76) and a fresh salad.

1 tablespoon vegetable oil
¾ cup finely diced onion
½ cup milk
1 egg, beaten
1½ cups The Lady & Sons Biscuit
   Mix

1 cup shredded sharp Cheddar
   cheese
½ teaspoon onion salt
2 tablespoons melted butter
1 tablespoon chopped fresh chives or
   parsley

Preheat the oven to 400 degrees. In a small skillet, heat the oil; sauté the onions until tender, about 2 minutes. Combine the milk and egg, and add to the Biscuit Mix along with the sautéed onions and ½ cup of the cheese. Stir only until the dry ingredients are just moistened. Spread the dough into a greased 8-inch round cake pan. Stir the onion salt into the butter. Drizzle this over the dough, and sprinkle with chives or parsley. Bake for 15 minutes, then sprinkle the dough with the remaining ½ cup cheese and return to the oven to bake for 5 minutes longer, or until golden brown. Cut the bread into wedges and serve hot with butter.

❦ ❦ ❦   *The Lady & Sons*

Riz Biscuits

YIELDS 18–24 BISCUITS

One ¼-ounce package dry yeast
1 cup warm buttermilk
½ teaspoon baking soda
2½ cups all-purpose flour
1 tablespoon sugar

1 teaspoon baking powder
¾ teaspoon salt
½ cup vegetable shortening
Melted butter

Dissolve the yeast in the milk; add the baking soda. Sift together the flour, sugar, baking powder, and salt. Cut the shortening into the flour with a fork. Stir the yeast mixture into the flour mixture with a spoon. Dust a rolling pin with additional flour and roll the dough out thin; brush with melted butter. Fold the dough over into a double thickness and brush the top with melted butter. Cut into rounds with a small biscuit cutter. Place the rounds of dough on a greased baking sheet and let rise for 1 hour. Preheat the oven to 425 degrees. Bake the biscuits for 10 to 12 minutes, or until lightly browned.

Blackberry Muffins

YIELDS 18 MUFFINS

½ cup (1 stick) melted butter
½ cup milk
2 large eggs, at room temperature
2 cups all-purpose flour
1¼ cups, plus 4 teaspoons sugar

2 teaspoons baking powder
½ teaspoon salt
2 cups fresh blackberries, or frozen
    blackberries, thawed and
    drained

Preheat the oven to 350 degrees. Grease eighteen 2½-inch muffin tins or line them with paper or foil liners. In a bowl, stir together the butter, milk, and eggs. In a mixing bowl, sift together the flour, 1¼ cups of the sugar, the baking powder, and the salt. Make a well in the center and pour in the milk mixture all at once; stir until blended. The batter will be lumpy: Do not overmix. Fold in the berries. Divide the batter among the prepared cups and sprinkle the remaining 4 teaspoons of sugar over the batter. Bake for about 25 minutes, or until golden.

Easy Herb Rolls

SERVES 6–8

One 12-ounce package
    refrigerated buttermilk biscuits
    (10 count)

¼ cup (½ stick) melted butter
2 tablespoons crumbled blue cheese
2 teaspoons dried parsley

1 teaspoon minced garlic

1 teaspoon minced chives

1 tablespoon onion flakes

1 teaspoon dried tarragon

½ teaspoon dried oregano

½ teaspoon celery seeds

Preheat oven to 375 degrees. Cut the biscuits into quarters. On a greased baking sheet arrange the biscuit pieces into an 11-inch-long loaf. It should resemble a loaf of French bread. In a small bowl, stir together the butter, blue cheese, parsley, garlic, chives, onion flakes, tarragon, oregano, and celery seeds. Spread the herbed butter over the loaf and bake for 18 to 20 minutes, or until golden.

Pineapple Upside-Down Biscuits

YIELDS 10 BISCUITS

One 10-ounce can crushed
   pineapple, drained, juice
   reserved
½ cup packed light brown sugar
¼ cup (½ stick) butter, at room
   temperature

10 maraschino cherries
One 12-ounce package
   refrigerated buttermilk biscuits
   (10 count)

Preheat the oven to 400 degrees. Grease 10 cups of a muffin tin. Combine the pineapple, sugar, and butter, and mix well. Divide the pineapple mixture among the muffin cups. Place a cherry in the center of each muffin cup. Place one biscuit in each cup on top of sugar and pineapple mixture. Spoon 1 teaspoon pineapple juice over each biscuit. Bake for 12 to 15 minutes, or until golden. Cool for 2 minutes. Invert the pan onto a plate to release the biscuits. Serve warm.

Green Muffins

YIELDS ABOUT 8 MUFFINS

Never miss the opportunity to make these when you have turnip greens left over from a previous meal.

1 cup self-rising cornmeal
½ cup self-rising flour
2 eggs
½ cup cooked turnip greens,
   chopped and drained, ½ cup pot
   liquor reserved

¼ cup vegetable oil
¼ cup sour cream

Preheat the oven to 350 degrees. Generously grease an 8-cup muffin tin and put it the oven to heat. In a mixing bowl, stir together the cornmeal and flour. Add the eggs, the greens and pot liquor, the oil, and sour cream. Divide the batter among the hot muffin cups. Bake for about 20 minutes. Serve the muffins hot with butter and a cup of pot liquor for dipping.

Sour Cream Butter Biscuits

YIELDS ABOUT 3 DOZEN MINIATURE BISCUITS

These biscuits take me back to my days at The Bag Lady. I would put a couple of these in each lunch container for an extra treat! They are wonderful.

2 cups self-rising flour
1 cup (2 sticks) butter, at room
   temperature

1 cup sour cream

Preheat the oven to 400 degrees. Mix the flour and butter together; add the sour cream, and blend well. Place spoonfuls of the batter in greased miniature muffin pans. Bake for 8 to 10 minutes, or until golden.

Old-Time Spoon Bread

SERVES 4–6

1½ cups water
1 teaspoon salt
1 cup cornmeal

3 tablespoons butter
2 eggs, separated
1 cup milk

Preheat the oven to 350 degrees. Bring the water to a boil and add the salt. Stir in the cornmeal and butter, then the egg yolks. Gradually stir in the milk. Beat the egg whites until stiff. Fold the egg whites into the cornmeal mixture. Pour the batter into a greased 2-quart casserole. Bake for 30 to 45 minutes, or until golden brown. Serve hot with gravy or butter.

Sweet Potato Biscuits

YIELDS 15–18 BISCUITS

¾ cup mashed cooked sweet
   potatoes
¼ cup milk
¼ cup (½ stick) butter

1¼ cups all-purpose flour
4 tablespoons baking powder
2 heaping tablespoons sugar
½ teaspoon salt

Preheat the oven to 450 degrees. In a large bowl, mix the potatoes, milk, and butter. In another bowl, sift together the flour, baking powder, sugar, and salt. Add the flour mixture to the potato mixture and combine to make a soft dough. Turn the dough out onto a floured board and toss lightly until the outside of the dough looks smooth. Roll the dough out to one-half inch thick and cut with a biscuit cutter. Place the biscuits on a greased pan and bake for about 15 minutes. (Watch your oven: If the biscuits are browning too fast, lower the temperature.)

Hush Puppies

YIELDS ABOUT 35 HUSH PUPPIES

6 cups vegetable oil
1½ cups self-rising cornmeal
½ cup self-rising flour
½ teaspoon baking soda

½ teaspoon salt
1 small onion, chopped
1 cup buttermilk
1 egg, lightly beaten

Prepare the oil for frying in a skillet. Preheat it to 350 degrees. In a mixing bowl, stir together the cornmeal, flour, baking soda, and salt. Stir in the onion. In a small bowl, stir together the buttermilk and egg. Pour the buttermilk mixture into the dry ingredients and mix until blended—don't worry if there are a few lumps. Drop the batter, one teaspoon at a time, into the oil. Dip the spoon in a glass of water after each hush puppy is dropped. Fry until golden brown, turning the hush puppies and during the cooking process.

VARIATION:For a sweet hush puppy, add 2 tablespoons sugar.

Apple Raisin Muffins

YIELDS ABOUT 5 DOZEN MINIATURE MUFFINS

2 cups water
2 cups sugar
2 cups grated apples
2 cups raisins
1 cup (2 sticks) butter
2 teaspoons cinnamon

2 teaspoons freshly grated nutmeg
½ teaspoon ground cloves
1 cup chopped walnuts
2 teaspoons baking soda
3½ cups all-purpose flour

Preheat the oven to 350 degrees. Combine the water, sugar, apples, raisins, butter, cinnamon, nutmeg, and cloves in a saucepan; bring to a boil. Remove the pan from the heat and cool completely.

In a large bowl, stir the nuts and baking soda into the flour. Add the cooled mixture to the bowl, and stir until blended. Fill greased miniature muffin tins with batter to the top. Bake for 15 minutes.

Gorilla Bread

SERVES 12–15

This bread kicks traditional monkey bread's butt! It's the best.

½ cup granulated sugar
3 teaspoons cinnamon
½ cup (1 stick) butter
1 cup packed brown sugar

One 8-ounce package cream cheese
Two 12-ounce cans refrigerated
 biscuits (10 count)
1½ cups coarsely chopped walnuts

Preheat the oven to 350 degrees. Spray a bundt pan with nonstick cooking spray. Mix the granulated sugar and cinnamon. In a saucepan, melt the butter and brown sugar over low heat, stirring well; set aside. Cut the cream cheese into 20 equal cubes. Press the biscuits out with your fingers and sprinkle each with ½ teaspoon of cinnamon sugar. Place a cube of cream cheese in the center of each biscuit, wrapping and sealing the dough around the cream cheese. Sprinkle ½ cup of the nuts into the bottom of the bundt pan. Place half of the prepared biscuits in the pan. Sprinkle with cinnamon sugar, pour half of the melted butter mixture over the biscuits, and sprinkle on ½ cup of nuts. Layer the remaining biscuits on top, sprinkle with the remaining cinnamon sugar, pour the remaining butter mixture over the biscuits, and sprinkle with the remaining ½ cup of nuts. Bake for 30 minutes. Remove from the oven and cool for 5 minutes. Place a plate on top and invert.

Nutty Orange Coffee Cake

SERVES 10–12

¾ cup granulated sugar
½ cup chopped pecans
2 teaspoons orange zest
Two 12-ounce cans refrigerated
 buttermilk biscuits (10 count)

One 8-ounce package cream cheese
½ cup (1 stick) melted butter
1 cup sifted confectioners' sugar
2 tablespoons fresh orange juice

Preheat the oven to 350 degrees. In a small bowl, combine the granulated sugar, pecans, and zest; set aside. Separate the biscuits. Place about ¾ teaspoon cream cheese in the center of each biscuit. Fold each biscuit in half over the cheese, pressing the edges to seal. Dip the biscuits in melted butter, then dredge in the granulated sugar mixture. Place the biscuits, curved-side down, in a single layer in the hollows of a lightly greased 12-cup bundt pan, spacing them evenly (do not stack). Place any remaining biscuits around the tube, filling in any gaps. Drizzle any remaining butter over the biscuits, and sprinkle with any remaining sugar mixture. Bake for 35 to 40 minutes, until golden brown. Immediately invert the cake onto a serving platter. Combine the confectioners' sugar and orange juice, stirring well; drizzle the glaze over the warm cake. Serve warm.

Cheesy French Bread

SERVES 6–8

One 8-ounce package shredded sharp Cheddar cheese or Mexican cheese blend
¾ cup mayonnaise

1½ teaspoons dried parsley flakes
⅛ teaspoon garlic powder
One 16-ounce loaf French bread, cut in half lengthwise

Combine the cheese, mayonnaise, parsley, and garlic powder, stirring well. Spread this mixture on the cut sides of the bread. Place the bread on a baking sheet and bake at 350 degrees for 15 to 20 minutes, or until the topping is melted and lightly browned.

Corny Corn Muffins

YIELDS 12 MUFFINS

In the restaurant, we serve our guests hot cheese biscuits and hoecake cornbread at lunchtime, but at dinner we swap out the hoecakes for these wonderful melt-in-your-mouth corn muffins.

1 cup self-rising cornmeal mix
¾ cup self-rising flour
½ cup vegetable oil
1 cup white creamed corn, fresh if
   possible, or frozen

2 eggs
1 cup sour cream
2 tablespoons sugar

Preheat oven to 375 degrees and grease a 12-cup muffin tin. (If you like a crispy edge around your muffins, preheat the tin in the oven until the grease is very hot.) Combine all ingredients and stir until moistened. Fill the muffin cups with batter and bake for 20 minutes or until golden brown.   ❧ ❧ ❧ *The Lady & Sons*

Banana Bread

YIELDS 1 LOAF

No electric mixer needed here—just mix in a bowl by hand.

½ cup (1 stick) butter, at room
   temperature
1 cup sugar
½ teaspoon salt
2 eggs

1 teaspoon vanilla extract
1½ cups all-purpose flour, sifted
1 teaspoon baking soda
1 teaspoon baking powder
3 ripe bananas, mashed

Preheat the oven to 350 degrees. Grease a 9 × 5-inch loaf pan. In a mixing bowl, combine the butter and sugar; mix well. Add the salt, eggs, vanilla, flour, baking soda, baking powder, and bananas, and mix well. Pour the batter into the prepared pan and bake for 50 minutes.

Sauces, Dressings, and Marinades

Southern Spice Rub

House Seasoning

Sweet and Sour Sauce

Wayne's Cranberry Sauce

Easy Homemade Blender Mayonnaise

Berry Steak Sauce

White Sauce

Mushroom Sauce

Tarragon Butter

Auntie's Peanut Sauce

Easy Hollandaise

Jezebel Sauce

Raspberry Sauce

Mocha Sauce

Peanut Butter Chocolate Sauce

Lime Vinaigrette

Warm Brie Salad Dressing

Balsamic Vinaigrette

Roasted Red Pepper Vinaigrette

Greek Salad Dressing

Southern Spice Rub

YIELDS ⅔ CUP

2 tablespoons ground cumin
2 tablespoons chili powder
1 tablespoon ground coriander
1 tablespoon kosher salt

2 teaspoons freshly ground pepper
½ teaspoon ground cinnamon
½ teaspoon red pepper flakes

Mix all of the ingredients in a small bowl. Sprinkle and rub the mixture on both sides of steaks just before grilling. Watch the meat while grilling: The spice rub should darken, but you don't want it to burn.

House Seasoning

YIELDS 1½ CUPS

1 cup salt
¼ cup black pepper

¼ cup garlic powder

Stir the ingredients together. Keep the seasoning in a shaker near the stove for convenience.   ❧ ❧ ❧   *The Lady & Sons*

Sweet and Sour Sauce

YIELDS ABOUT 1¾ CUPS

1 cup sugar
½ cup white vinegar
½ cup, plus 1 tablespoon water
1 tablespoon chopped green bell
   pepper

1 tablespoon chopped pimentos
½ teaspoon salt
2 teaspoons cornstarch
1 teaspoon paprika

In a saucepan combine the sugar, vinegar, the ½ cup of water, bell pepper, pimento, and salt; simmer for 5 minutes. Stir together the cornstarch and the remaining 1 tablespoon water. Add this to the vinegar mixture; remove the pan from the heat and stir until thick. Add the paprika and let cool completely. Serve with fried shrimp, fried chicken bites, or pork bites.

Wayne's Cranberry Sauce

YIELDS 4–5 CUPS

1 cup sugar
1 cup water
One 16-ounce bag fresh
   cranberries
1 cup chopped apple
1 cup chopped walnuts

½ cup raisins
¼ cup Grand Marnier
Juice of ½ orange
Juice of ½ lemon
1 teaspoon cinnamon
1 teaspoon freshly grated nutmeg

Combine the sugar and water in a large saucepan and bring to a boil. Add the cranberries and return to a boil, then lower the heat so that the liquid simmers. Add the apple, walnuts, raisins, Grand Marnier, orange and lemon juices, cinnamon, and nutmeg, and cook for 10 to 15 minutes. Remove the pan from the heat and let the sauce cool.

Easy Homemade Blender Mayonnaise

YIELDS 1 CUP

1 cup vegetable oil
1 egg
3 teaspoons fresh lemon juice

¾ teaspoon salt
½ teaspoon dry mustard
1 tablespoon hot water

In the container of a blender, combine ¼ cup of the oil, the egg, lemon juice, salt, and mustard, and blend for just a few seconds. With the blender running, drizzle in the remaining ¾ cup oil. Blend in the hot water.

Berry Steak Sauce

YIELDS 2 CUPS

One 16-ounce can jellied
  cranberry sauce
⅓ cup bottled steak sauce

1 tablespoon brown sugar
1 tablespoon vegetable oil
2 teaspoons prepared mustard

Combine all the ingredients in a mixing bowl and beat with an electric mixer until smooth. Serve hot or cold, with pork, beef, or chicken.

White Sauce

YIELDS 1 CUP

To make a tasty cheese sauce for vegetables, add ½ cup shredded cheese.

2 tablespoons butter
2 tablespoons all-purpose flour
¼ teaspoon salt

Pinch of white pepper
1 cup milk

Melt the butter in a saucepan over medium heat. Whisk in the flour, salt, and pepper. Add the milk all at once, and cook quickly, stirring constantly, until the sauce is thick and creamy.

Mushroom Sauce

YIELDS ABOUT 2 CUPS

3 tablespoons butter
½ pound fresh mushrooms,
   trimmed and sliced
1 tablespoon all-purpose flour

1 teaspoon soy sauce
¾ cup half-and-half
The Lady's House Seasoning

Melt the butter in a skillet. Add the mushrooms, sprinkle in the flour, and stir well. Cook over medium heat for 8 to 10 minutes, stirring as needed. Add the soy sauce, then slowly stir in the half-and-half. Cook and stir until the sauce thickens. Season to taste with House Seasoning. This sauce is delicious with steak.

Tarragon Butter

YIELDS 1 STICK (½ CUP)

½ cup (1 stick) butter, at room
   temperature
1 tablespoon minced fresh
   tarragon

1 teaspoon fresh lemon juice

Beat the butter with an electric mixer until fluffy, then stir in the tarragon and lemon juice. Using waxed paper, shape the butter into a log. (If you want to pipe the butter into decorative shapes, spoon it into a pastry bag fitted with a star tip.) Chill. Slice the butter log and place a few slices on top of grilled steak or fish.

Auntie's Peanut Sauce

YIELDS 1¾ CUPS

This is excellent on char-grilled chicken or pork. Swab or brush the sauce on the meat for the last 15 minutes of grilling time. Turn often, continuing to baste, to prevent burning.

½ cup (1 stick) butter
2 large cloves garlic, crushed
1 cup Worcestershire sauce

¼ cup crunchy peanut butter
Juice of 2 lemons
½ teaspoon black pepper

Heat the butter in a skillet. Add the garlic and sauté, being careful not to burn the garlic. Add the Worcestershire sauce, peanut butter, lemon juice, and pepper, and blend well. Simmer for 10 minutes.

❦ ❦ ❦ *The Lady & Sons*

Easy Hollandaise

YIELDS ⅔ CUP

½ cup (1 stick) butter
3 egg yolks

3 tablespoons fresh lemon juice

Combine the ingredients in a small saucepan and let stand at room temperature until the butter is soft (45 to 60 minutes). Five minutes before serving time, place the saucepan over low heat, and stir constantly until the sauce thickens.

Jezebel Sauce

YIELDS 3½ CUPS

One 12-ounce bag frozen
   cranberries
½ cup, plus 2 tablespoons prepared
   horseradish

3 tablespoons dry mustard
1 tablespoon coarsely ground
   pepper

Combine all the ingredients in a large bowl and stir well. Pour the sauce into an airtight container and store in the refrigerator. Serve with crackers and cream cheese, as an appetizer, or along with chicken, pork, or beef.   ❧ ❧ ❧ **The Lady & Sons**

Raspberry Sauce

YIELDS ABOUT 2½ CUPS

This sauce makes something special out of plain cake or vanilla ice cream.

One 10-ounce package frozen
   raspberries, thawed
½ cup currant jelly

1 tablespoon cornstarch
1 tablespoon butter
¾ cup fresh orange juice

In a saucepan, mix ¾ cup of the raspberries with the jelly and bring to a boil. Reduce the heat. Stir the cornstarch into the remaining raspberries and add this to the saucepan; cook, stirring constantly, until thickened. Remove the pan from the heat and stir in the butter. Cool. Stir in the orange juice and refrigerate until chilled.

Mocha Sauce

YIELDS 1 CUP

This sauce is wonderful on pound cake, ice cream, and many other desserts.

½ cup unsweetened cocoa powder   ½ cup honey
½ cup strong brewed coffee   ¼ cup heavy cream

In a small saucepan, combine all the ingredients and cook over medium heat, stirring constantly, until the mixture is smooth and slightly thickened. Cool.

Peanut Butter Chocolate Sauce

YIELDS 2⅔ CUPS

One 13-ounce can evaporated milk   ½ cup creamy peanut butter
2 cups sugar   1 teaspoon vanilla extract
3 squares (3 ounces) unsweetened
   chocolate

In a medium saucepan, combine the milk, sugar, and chocolate. Bring to a boil over low heat, stirring until the sugar is dissolved and chocolate is melted. Boil gently, stirring occasionally, for 15 minutes. Remove the pan from the heat and stir in the peanut butter and vanilla; beat until blended. Serve warm. This sauce keeps well in the refrigerator, but it will thicken when chilled. To serve, spoon the desired amount of sauce into a saucepan; place over low heat and stir until warm and pourable.

Lime Vinaigrette

YIELDS 2⅓ CUPS

¾ *cup olive oil*
¾ *cup vegetable oil*
½ *cup red wine vinegar*
1½ *tablespoons Dijon mustard*
1½ *tablespoons fresh lime juice*
1½ *tablespoons crushed garlic*
1½ *tablespoons soy sauce*

Pinch of dried thyme
Pinch of dried basil
Pinch of dried oregano
Pinch of dried dillweed
Pinch of salt
Pinch of pepper

Combine all the ingredients in the container of a blender and blend until thick and smooth. This dressing may be stored in the refrigerator in a tightly closed jar for up to 2 weeks.

Warm Brie Salad Dressing

YIELDS ABOUT 1¼ CUPS

Pour this dressing over mixed greens such as Romaine, Boston, and one or two types of bitter greens.

2 *tablespoons olive oil*
1 *green onion, finely chopped*
½ *pound Brie*
2 *tablespoons coarse Dijon*
  mustard

3 *tablespoons sherry vinegar or*
  raspberry vinegar
1 *tablespoon capers (optional)*
Salt and pepper

Heat the oil in a saucepan over low heat. Add the onion and cook until softened. Meanwhile, use a paring knife to remove the rind from the Brie. Add the mustard to the suacepan, then the vinegar, and stir well. Add the Brie and mix until smooth; let cool slightly, then add the capers, if using. Add salt and pepper to taste.

Balsamic Vinaigrette

YIELDS 1⅓ CUPS

This dressing is especially good on tossed greens with tomatoes, red onion, and crumbled blue cheese.

1 cup olive oil
¼ cup balsamic vinegar
2 tablespoons sugar

2 large cloves garlic, crushed
1 teaspoon salt
½ teaspoon pepper

Combine all the ingredients in a jar with a tight-fitting lid and shake well. Let stand for at least ½ hour before using.

Roasted Red Pepper Vinaigrette

YIELDS 2–2½ CUPS

This is great over salad greens and excellent with fish; you can also use it as a light veggie dip. I recommend roasting fresh red bell peppers, but if time doesn't allow, substitute a 14-ounce jar of roasted red peppers, drained, adding 1 teaspoon of sugar to ensure sweetness.

4 red bell peppers
¼ cup balsamic vinegar
1 tablespoon minced garlic

¾ cup olive oil
Salt and pepper

Roast the bell peppers under the broiler, or bake them on a baking sheet in a 500-degree oven for 10 to 12 minutes, or until the skins are blackened. Place the charred peppers in a paper bag, close the top, and let the peppers cool for 10 minutes. When the peppers are cool, rub off the charred skin and rinse under cold water. Stem and seed the peppers. In a food processor or blender, purée the peppers to a fine consistency. Add the vinegar and garlic and process on low speed, slowly drizzling in the oil. Add salt and pepper to taste.

❧ ❧ ❧ **The Lady & Sons**

Greek Salad Dressing

YIELDS 1 CUP

¼ cup balsamic vinegar
3 tablespoons water
One 0.7-ounce package Good
   Seasons Italian Salad Dressing
   Mix

1 teaspoon anchovy paste (from a
   tube)
½ cup extra-virgin olive oil

Whisk together the vinegar, water, dressing mix, and anchovy paste. Add the oil and whisk until blended.

And from My Peers . . .

HERB TRAUB AND THE PIRATES' HOUSE

Ring Tum Ditty

Gussie's Fried Chicken with Pecan-Honey Glaze

Green Beans with Onions

THE GRANITE STEPS INN

French Toast Stuffed with Bananas and Walnuts

Lemon-Pecan Sunburst Coffee Cake

Oven-Baked Dutch Apple Pancake

DAMON LEE FOWLER

Turnips Stuffed with Winter Greens

Asparagus with Leeks and New Potatoes

Watermelon Salad

MARTHA GIDDENS NESBIT

Mosaic Chicken Terrine

Crab Cakes with Lemon Dill Sauce

Mrs. Sullivan's Benne Wafers

THE GASTONIAN

Traditional Raisin Scones

Strawberry Soup

Pesto Cheese Blossom

MRS. WILKES' BOARDING HOUSE

Mrs. Wilkes' Boarding House–Style Biscuits

Baked Bean Casserole

Beef Stew Casserole

ELIZABETH ON 37TH

Fried Grits Cakes with Sausage

Shrimp Bel Vedere

Blueberry Raspberry Pecan Crisp

THE JOHNNY HARRIS RESTAURANT

Steak au Poivre

Baked Flounder

Pasta Puttanesca Sauce

LUCILE WRIGHT

Lucile Wright's Tomato Sandwiches

Lucile Wright's Oyster Bisque

JOHN BERENDT

Fresh Cabbage and Sweet Sausages
Lemon Hollandaise Sauce
Pots de Crème

THERE ARE so many things of interest here in our beautiful city of Savannah—too many to mention in just one book. Our city is full of restaurants, old and new, offering a variety of cuisines. She has more than two dozen antique-filled inns gracing the historic district, and literally wraps her arms around us with rich history and great beauty.

In this chapter I have included recipes from two inns located near my home, four restaurants that have brought pleasure to their guests for years, two local (and very successful) cookbook authors, and one caterer.

Thank you all so much for your contributions to this book. They are truly the icing on the cake.

Herb Traub and the Pirates' House

For years Herb Traub was known as one of the most hospitable and gracious hosts in Savannah. He was the proprietor of the legendary Pirates' House, located in one of the most historic spots in Georgia, on the site of the Trustees' Garden, the first public experimental garden in America.

When General James Edward Oglethorpe arrived here from England in 1733, he established this large garden on what was then the edge of the city, and he named it in honor of his fellow Englishmen who were the Trustees of the infant colony of Georgia. By the middle of the eighteenth century, the need for the garden no longer existed, and it soon became the site of some of Savannah's earliest construction. Located just yards from the Savannah River, it was a natural spot for an inn for visiting sailors. The inn soon became a rendezvous for bloodthirsty pirates from around the world. It is said that Old Cap'n Flint died in one of the rooms upstairs, and on moonless nights his ghost still haunts the grounds of the Pirates' House.

Today the inn is home to a bustling restaurant—a meandering maze of twenty-three dining rooms in nine connected old buildings. Upstairs is one of Savannah's favorite nightspots, Hannah's East, where Savannah's own Ben Tucker pours out a healthy helping of jazz. Hannah's East is also where our dear, sweet "Miss" Emma Kelley, "The Lady of 6,000 Songs," can be found stroking the ivories and singing some of my favorite tunes.

Herb published *The Pirates' House Cookbook* in 1982, and while he is no longer involved in the restaurant, his cookbook has remained ever so popular. He always has a smile and I can just hear him saying, "What foods these morsels be."

Thank you for your contribution to my cookbook, Herb!

Ring Tum Ditty

SERVES 4 HOGOLETTOS (OR 6 NORMAL PEOPLE)

12 ounces bacon, chopped
2 cups chopped onions
Two 16-ounce cans whole tomatoes, juice reserved
One 16-ounce can whole kernel corn

Dried basil
Salt and pepper
3 cups (¾ pound) grated extra-sharp Cheddar cheese
4–6 baking potatoes, baked

Sauté the bacon and onions in a heavy pot until the bacon is crisp and the onion is translucent. Drain off the fat. Drain the tomato juice into the pot; squish the tomatoes through your fingers into the pot. Add the corn, and basil, salt, and pepper to taste, and simmer the mixture for 10 to 15 minutes or until desired thickness. Add the cheese and stir until melted. Spoon the Ring Tum Ditty over the halved potatoes and wait for the compliments.

Gussie's Fried Chicken with Pecan-Honey Glaze

SERVES 4

They use deep-fat fryers at the Pirates' House. If you have one at home, by all means use it.

3–3½ pounds frying chicken, cut up, or your favorite chicken parts
2 eggs
Salt and pepper
Garlic powder
Vegetable shortening or vegetable oil

2 cups self-rising flour
1 cup (2 sticks) butter
½ cup honey
½ cup coarsely chopped pecans

Rinse the chicken and pat it dry. Beat the eggs in a 9 × 13-inch dish. Lay the chicken pieces in the dish, and sprinkle with salt, pepper, and garlic powder to taste. Turn the chicken and season the other side, then slosh the chicken parts around in the egg until well coated. Place enough shortening or oil in a cast-iron skillet or electric skillet to come just over halfway up the sides of the chicken parts. Heat just until smoking (375 degrees). Place the flour in a paper bag, add the chicken pieces, a few at a time, and shake to coat well. Remove the chicken with tongs and place it in the hot fat. Cover the pan, leaving a crack for steam to escape, lower the heat (to 325 degrees for electric skillet), and cook for 10 minutes. Turn the chicken with tongs, cover again (leaving the lid open just a crack), and cook for 10 minutes longer. Very large pieces may need to be cooked a little longer. Drain the chicken on paper towels and transfer to a platter.

To make the glaze, melt the butter in a saucepan over low heat. Whisk in the honey until well blended. Bring to a simmer and add the pecans. Simmer for 15 minutes, stirring occasionally. Ladle the glaze over the hot fried chicken and serve.

Green Beans with Onions

SERVES 6

2½–3 pounds string beans	*1 small onion, peeled and cut into*
4 slices thick bacon or 4 tablespoons	*thin wedges*
bacon fat	*Salt and pepper*
1 tablespoon sugar	

With a paring knife or peeler, trim the edges off the beans to remove the strings. Do not omit this step—you can do it while watching TV or chatting with a friend. Place the bacon in a heavy Dutch oven and cook over low heat to render some of the fat; do not brown. (If using bacon fat, just melt it.) Meanwhile, wash the beans. Then hold a handful at a time under vigorously running cold water and drop the wet beans directly into the Dutch oven. Sprinkle the beans with sugar; do not add water. Bring to a boil, cover the pot, and immediately reduce the heat to low. Cook until the beans are tender, 45 to 60 minutes. Add a little more water if necessary. During the last 30 minutes of cooking, place the onions around the edge of the pot. When the beans are done, season to taste with salt and pepper. (Do not add salt at the beginning, or the beans may be too salty.)

The Granite Steps Inn

This beautiful mansion is located at 126 East Gaston Street. The Granite Steps Mansion was a private residence until 1998, making it one of the "newest" old bed-and-breakfasts in Savannah. The innkeeper, Donna Panoz Sparks, and I became fast friends. Donna and her mother, Nancy Panoz, are two of the most genial ladies you could ever meet. These two are no strangers to seeing to the comfort of others. They have a proven recipe for true "quality of life" in their winery and resort, the Chateau Élan, located in the hills of northern Georgia. The Chateau offers a welcoming refuge rich in old-world tradition and warm hospitality—qualities that also characterize the Granite Steps Inn.

Along with some favorite recipes served at the Inn, Donna sends this message to everyone: "It is an unbelievable honor to be able to establish a bed-and-breakfast inn in Savannah. Apart from being the most beautiful city in the United States, Savannah has welcomed us with open arms. In return, we want to provide Savannah with one of the finest bed-and-breakfast inns available anywhere. The Granite Steps has provided the perfect backdrop for this. It is a grand and elegant house that beckons people to come inside. However, once they are inside, we hope to provide our guests with the kind of warm hospitality that is the essence of Savannah. We like to call it 'white-glove service without the white gloves.'"

French Toast Stuffed with Bananas and Walnuts

SERVES 4

Sandwiching two slices of bread with a mixture of bananas and walnuts results in French toast with a surprise filling. Try other favorite nuts in place of the walnuts, if you like. Accompany the French toast with bacon, ham, or sausage.

6 eggs

¼ cup milk

4 very ripe bananas

¼ cup (1 ounce) coarsely chopped
    walnuts

⅛ teaspoon freshly grated nutmeg

8 slices egg bread

4 tablespoons (½ stick) unsalted
    butter

Confectioners' sugar, for dusting

In a large, shallow bowl, using a fork, beat the eggs until lightly frothy. Stir in the milk; set aside. Peel the bananas into a small bowl and mash them with a fork. Stir in the walnuts and nutmeg. Spread the banana-walnut mixture evenly over half the bread slices, leaving a ¼-inch border uncovered on all edges. Top with the remaining bread slices and press down gently to seal. Place 2 sandwiches in the egg mixture and press down gently. Turn gently and let soak for a moment, until evenly saturated on both sides. Remove from the bowl and repeat with the remaining 2 sandwiches. In a frying pan or on a griddle large enough to hold all the sandwiches at once, melt 2 tablespoons of the butter over medium heat. Add the sandwiches and fry until the undersides are golden brown, about 2 minutes. Cut the remaining 2 tablespoons butter into several pieces and dot them around the pan. Flip the sandwiches with a spatula and fry until the second side is browned, about 2 minutes longer. Place the French toast on warmed individual plates. Using a small, fine sieve, lightly dust the tops with confectioners' sugar. Serve hot, with jam or maple syrup.

Lemon-Pecan Sunburst Coffee Cake

SERVES 8

One 17.3-ounce can refrigerated
    Pillsbury Grands Flaky Biscuits

¼ cup finely chopped pecans

¼ cup granulated sugar

2 teaspoons grated lemon zest

2 tablespoons melted butter

½ cup confectioners' sugar

1½ ounces cream cheese, at room
    temperature

2½–3 teaspoons fresh lemon juice

Preheat the oven to 375 degrees. Grease a 9- or 8-inch round cake pan. Separate the biscuit dough into 8 biscuits. Place one biscuit in the center of the pan. Cut the remaining biscuits in half, forming 14 half-circles. Arrange these pieces around the center biscuit in a sunburst pattern, with all the cut sides facing in the same direction. In a small bowl, combine the pecans, granulated sugar, and lemon zest, and mix well. Brush the tops of the biscuits with the melted butter and sprinkle with the pecan mixture. Bake for 20 to 25 minutes, or until golden brown. Meanwhile, in a small bowl, combine the confectioners' sugar, cream cheese, and enough lemon juice to make a pourable glaze; beat until smooth. Drizzle the glaze over the warm coffee cake. Let stand for 10 minutes, or just until the glaze is set. Serve warm.

Oven-Baked Dutch Apple Pancakes

SERVES 4–6

2 cans apple pie filling
2 tablespoons butter
1 teaspoon cinnamon
3 eggs
½ cup milk

½ cup all-purpose flour
1 tablespoon sour cream
1 teaspoon lemon zest
¼ teaspoon salt
Confectioners' sugar, for dusting

Preheat the oven to 350 degrees. In a 10-inch cast-iron skillet, warm the apple pie filling, butter, and cinnamon. In a bowl, beat the eggs until frothy. Add the milk, flour, sour cream, lemon zest, and salt. Beat just until the batter is smooth. Pour over the hot apple mixture in the skillet, and immediately put the pan in the oven. Bake for 20 to 25 minutes, or until the pancake is puffed and golden brown. Using a small, fine sieve, lightly dust the top of the pancake with confectioners' sugar. Serve warm.

Damon Lee Fowler

My friend Damon is a nationally recognized authority on Southern cooking and its history. He received a master's degree in architecture from Clemson University, after which he practiced as an architect for more than a decade before turning to his true loves: food writing, teaching, and culinary history. I always enjoy my time spent with Damon; he's so knowledgeable, and funny as all get-out.

Damon has authored three cookbooks. His first, *Classical Southern Cooking: A Celebration of the Cuisine of the Old South,* was nominated for two Julia Child Cookbook Awards and a James Beard Foundation Award. His second book, *Beans, Greens, and Sweet Georgia Peaches,* explores Southern fruit and vegetable cookery. His last was simply called *Fried Chicken.*

He has shared with us three recipes from his book *Beans, Greens, and Sweet Georgia Peaches.* I hope you enjoy them.

Turnips Stuffed with Winter Greens

SERVES 4

4 large turnips (about 2 pounds)
4 tablespoons (½ stick) unsalted
  butter, plus more for greasing
1 pound kale or young collards
½ cup dry breadcrumbs

Grated zest of 1 lemon
4 green onions, thinly sliced
Salt and freshly ground black
  pepper

Position a rack in the upper third of the oven and preheat the oven to 400 degrees. Trim most of the taproots and green tops from the turnips, but leave a little of both attached. Scrub the turnips well under cold running water and pat dry. Rub them with a little butter, wrap them in foil, and put them on a baking sheet. Place the baking sheet on the upper rack of the oven and bake until the turnips yield slightly when pressed with a finger, about 1 hour.

Meanwhile, stem the greens and cut them into 1-inch-wide strips. Wash them thoroughly and drain them, leaving some moisture clinging to the leaves. Put the greens in a large skillet, cover, and cook over medium-high heat until the greens are wilted but still bright green, about 4 minutes. Turn the greens out onto a platter and spread them out to cool.

Melt 2 tablespoons of the butter in a small pan over medium heat. Add the breadcrumbs and lemon zest, and thoroughly mix them with the butter. Transfer the mixture to a bowl and set aside.

When the turnips are tender, unwrap them and let them stand until cool enough to handle. Slice off the tops; then, with a melon baller or a small spoon, scoop out the inner flesh, leaving a ½-inch-thick shell. Set aside the inner flesh for another use. Put the shells on a lightly greased baking sheet and set aside.

Put the onions and the remaining 2 tablespoons of butter in the skillet used to cook the greens, and place over medium-high heat. Sauté until the onions are softened, about 2 minutes. Add the greens, a liberal pinch of salt, and a few grindings of pepper, and toss well. Fill the turnips with the greens, sprinkle them with the crumb mixture, and bake until the crumbs are golden and the turnips and greens are heated through, about 20 minutes.

Asparagus with Leeks and New Potatoes

SERVES 4

1½ pounds fresh asparagus, peeled and trimmed
Green tops of 2 large leeks, washed and trimmed
½ pound small new red potatoes, cooked but not peeled

4 tablespoons (½ stick) unsalted butter
Salt and freshly ground pepper

Cut the asparagus crosswise into 1-inch lengths, keeping the tips separate from the stems; set aside. Slice the leek tops crosswise about ¼ inch thick. Slice the potatoes into ¼-inch-thick rounds.

In a skillet or sauté pan that will comfortably hold all the ingredients, melt the butter over medium-high heat. Add the potatoes and the asparagus stems. Sauté, shaking the pan frequently, until the potatoes are beginning to turn golden, about 3 minutes.

Add the leek greens and asparagus tips, a healthy pinch of salt, and a liberal grinding of pepper. Sauté, shaking the pan and tossing the ingredients frequently, until the asparagus is tender and beginning to brown a little. It should still be firm and bright green. Taste and correct the seasonings, and serve at once.

Watermelon Salad

SERVES 6

Here, watermelon gives up its usual place at the table as a fruit and goes to work in a role usually occupied by its cousin, the cucumber. The melon is a lovely foil for the salty feta, tangy onion, and tart vinegar. It makes a refreshing and unusual salad for any summer brunch, luncheon, or dinner.

½ small watermelon (about 5 pounds)
1 medium Vidalia or other sweet onion
¼ cup red wine vinegar
Salt and freshly ground black pepper

½ cup extra-virgin olive oil
2 tablespoons chopped fresh mint
4 ounces feta cheese, crumbled
6 whole mint sprigs, for garnish

Cut the flesh from the melon and cut it into bite-size pieces, removing and discarding the seeds as you go; set aside. Peel and slice the onion into thin rings.

In a bowl, combine the vinegar, a large pinch of salt, and a few liberal grindings of pepper, and whisk until the salt is dissolved. Slowly whisk in the oil, a few drops at a time. Stir in the chopped mint, taste, and correct the seasonings.

Combine the melon, onion, and feta in a bowl, pour the dressing over them, and toss gently until they are coated and evenly mixed. Garnish with the mint sprigs, or divide the salad among individual salad plates and garnish each serving. Serve at once.

Martha Giddens Nesbit

Since her graduation twenty-five years ago, Martha has worked in various capacities at the Savannah *Morning News*—as columnist, food editor, and lifestyle editor. She writes regularly for the Accent/Food section, and is a regular contributor to *Savannah Magazine*. Martha has been the recipient of many national awards for fashion and nutrition reporting.

In 1986 Martha self-published a cookbook called *Savannah Collection,* five years later she wrote *Savannah, Crown of the Colonial Coast,* and last but not least, in 1996 she came out with *Savannah Entertains.*

Over the years my respect for Martha has grown with everything she's done. I know everyone will enjoy the recipes that she has contributed from her own cookbooks. Thanks, Martha!

Mosaic Chicken Terrine

SERVES 12–14

2 eggs, lightly beaten
½ teaspoon lemon pepper
½ teaspoon Lawry's Seasoned Salt
1½ pounds boneless chicken breast
   halves
2 cups grated Parmesan
One 14½-ounce can artichoke
   hearts, drained and cut in half
6 slices mortadella, salami, or
   prosciutto

12–16 large fresh basil leaves, or
   8 spinach leaves
1 cup mayonnaise
½ clove garlic, minced
1 teaspoon fresh dillweed, or
   ½ teaspoon dried
1 teaspoon chopped fresh parsley

Beat the eggs in a small bowl and add the lemon pepper and Seasoned Salt. Dip the chicken breasts into the eggs, then into the Parmesan. Dip the artichoke hearts into the eggs, then into the Parmesan.

Line a large loaf pan with parchment paper. Place one layer of chicken breasts on the bottom of the pan (this will use about 2½ breasts). Cover the chicken with a layer of mortadella, salami, or prosciutto. Cover the ham with a layer of artichoke hearts, then cover with the basil leaves, using all the leaves. Repeat the layers of chicken, ham, and artichoke hearts. Cover the top of the terrine with parchment paper or foil. During baking, the terrine must be weighted with something heavy to compress the layers. A clean brick wrapped in foil works nicely and fits nicely in loaf pan. Put the loaf pan in a larger baking pan, and pour in water to a depth of 1½ inches. Bake at 350 degrees for 1 hour and 20 minutes.

Let the terrine cool completely at room temperature, then refrigerate in the loaf pan for several hours, or overnight. In a bowl, blend the mayonnaise, garlic, dillweed, and parsley with a spoon; chill. To serve, carefully turn the terrine out of the pan onto a platter and cut ¾-inch slices. Serve with mayonnaise mixture and good buttery crackers.

Crab Cakes with Lemon Dill Sauce

SERVES 4

3 tablespoons butter
1 green onion, finely chopped
2 tablespoons finely chopped red
   bell pepper
1 clove garlic, minced
3 tablespoons heavy cream
1 tablespoon Dijon mustard
Cayenne pepper

1 cup breadcrumbs
1 egg
½ teaspoon minced fresh parsley
1 pound white or claw crabmeat,
   picked free of any bits of shell
¼ cup grated Parmesan
2 tablespoons vegetable oil

Melt 1 tablespoon of the butter in a heavy skillet over medium heat. Sauté the onion, bell pepper, and garlic in the butter until the pepper is limp, about 3 minutes. Add the cream, mustard, and cayenne to taste, and mix well. Add ½ cup of the breadcrumbs, the egg, and the parsley, and mix well. Gently fold in the crabmeat.

Form the mixture into 8 patties, about ½ inch thick. Combine the remaining ½ cup breadcrumbs and the Parmesan in a bowl; pat this topping onto both sides of the patties. Refrigerate until firm, about 2 hours.

Combine the oil and the remaining 2 tablespoons of butter in the skillet. Sauté the crab cakes in the hot oil-butter mixture for about 3 minutes on each side, or until golden brown. Or, place the crab cakes on a baking sheet, drizzle with the oil and butter mixture, and bake at 400 degrees for 7 to 10 minutes, turning once.

Spoon a dollop of Lemon Dill Sauce alongside each crab cake, and serve the remaining sauce separately.

LEMON DILL SAUCE

YIELDS ABOUT 1½ CUPS

1 cup mayonnaise
¼ cup buttermilk
2 tablespoons chopped fresh dill
1 tablespoon minced fresh parsley

1 tablespoon grated lemon zest
2 teaspoons fresh lemon juice
1 small garlic clove, minced

Combine all the ingredients in a bowl and stir well. Refrigerate until chilled; the sauce will thicken as it chills.

Mrs. Sullivan's Benne Wafers

YIELDS ABOUT 12 DOZEN WAFERS

1½ cups sesame seeds, toasted
2 cups all-purpose flour
1 teaspoon baking powder
¼ teaspoon salt

1½ cups (3 sticks) butter
1 pound light brown sugar
2 eggs
2 teaspoons vanilla extract

Line some baking sheets with waxed paper. Preheat the oven to 350 degrees. To toast the sesame seeds, spread them in a shallow baking pan. Bake for about 5 minutes, watching carefully. The seeds should just begin to lightly brown. Immediately tip the seeds into a shallow dish and set aside to cool. Reduce the oven temperature to 300 degrees.

Sift together the flour, baking powder, and salt. In a mixing bowl, cream together the butter and sugar. Beat in the eggs. Stir in the flour mixture until combined, then add the vanilla. Stir in the sesame seeds. Drop by ½ teaspoons on the prepared baking sheets.

Bake until brown, 14 to 16 minutes. The cookies should be very brown, but not burned around the edges. Let the cookies cool completely on the waxed paper, then lift them off. Store the wafers in an airtight container. These freeze well in tins.

The Gastonian

The Gastonian is located at 220 East Gaston Street in Savannah's beautiful historic district. Anne Landers, owner and innkeeper, has a gift for making people feel welcome in this breathtaking 1868 Regency-Italianate-style home.

This beautiful inn has been the recipient of many awards, among them being named one of the top inns and bed-and-breakfasts in the United States by the Zagat survey.

The Gastonian was selected as one of the twelve most romantic inns on the East Coast by *The Discerning Traveler* and also boasts the prestigious AAA "Four Diamond Award."

Anne, along with her full-time pastry chef, Laura Steele, has been gracious enough to share a few of their sumptuous recipes. The recipes that Anne and Laura selected for us are prepared and served at High Tea every afternoon at the inn. Thank you, ladies, for your generosity.

Traditional Raisin Scones

YIELDS 1 DOZEN SCONES

3 cups all-purpose flour
1 tablespoon baking powder
1 cup (2 sticks) unsalted butter, at room temperature
¼ cup, plus 2 tablespoons sugar
3 large eggs
⅓ cup buttermilk
½ cup raisins

Preheat the oven to 350 degrees. Sift together the flour and baking powder. In a separate bowl, beat the butter until creamy. Add the ¼ cup sugar, beating until pale and fluffy. Add the eggs, one at a time, then add the flour mixture and the buttermilk. Sprinkle the raisins over the dough and gently fold them in. Using an ice-cream scoop, place mounds of dough on a baking sheet and sprinkle with the remaining sugar. Bake for 30 minutes. Serve the scones warm, with softened butter and preserves.

Strawberry Soup

SERVES 6–8

1 quart strawberries, hulled
4 cups buttermilk
¾ cup sugar

⅔ cup sour cream
3 tablespoons peach schnapps
Fresh mint sprigs

In the bowl of a food processor, combine the strawberries, 1 cup of the buttermilk, and the sugar. Process until blended and set aside. Combine the remaining 3 cups of buttermilk, the sour cream, and schnapps in a large bowl. Pour the strawberry mixture into the sour cream mixture and stir to combine. Cover and refrigerate until well chilled. Serve the soup chilled in small cups, garnished with mint sprigs.

Pesto Cheese Blossom

SERVES 15–20

One 8-ounce package sliced
  provolone cheese
Two 8-ounce packages cream
  cheese, at room temperature
20 pistachios, shelled
2 cloves garlic
½ cup fresh basil leaves

½ cup fresh parsley leaves
½ cup pine nuts
¼ teaspoon salt
¼ teaspoon freshly ground pepper
2 tablespoons extra-virgin olive oil
3 ounces oil-packed sun-dried
  tomatoes*

Line a medium bowl with plastic wrap, leaving enough overhang to cover the top. Reserving 3 slices of the provolone, line the bottom and sides of the bowl with the remaining provolone, overlapping the slices. For the cream cheese layer, process the cream cheese, pistachios, and 1 of the garlic cloves in a food processor until blended; scrape the mixture into a bowl and set aside. For the pesto layer, process the basil, parsley, pine nuts, and the remaining garlic clove in the food processor

---

*If you can't get oil-packed sun-dried tomatoes, use the dry-packed kind. Reconstitute them by placing the tomatoes in a small saucepan, adding a little olive oil and water, and cooking, covered, for 3 minutes.

until blended. Dissolve the salt and pepper in the olive oil and mix well. With the machine running, add the oil in a fine stream. Scrape this mixture into a second bowl and set aside. For the tomato layer, drain the tomatoes, reserving the oil. Purée the tomatoes with a small amount of the reserved oil in a food processor. Spread some of the cream cheese mixture over the cheese slices lining the bowl. Layer the pesto mixture, half of the remaining cream cheese mixture, the sun-dried tomato mixture, and then remaining cream cheese mixture in the bowl. Cover with the remaining provolone cheese. Bring the edges of the plastic wrap together over the top and secure with a twist tie. Freeze until firm.

Remove the plastic wrap and invert the mold onto a serving platter. Serve with party crackers. This will keep in the refrigerator for up to 3 months.

Mrs. Wilkes' Boarding House

Although Mrs. Sema Wilkes and my grandmother Irene Paul never met, they had a lot in common. Mrs. Wilkes is, and my grandmother was, a wonderful Southern cook. They both began their businesses in the early 1940s, before it was fashionable for women to be in the business world. Today, fifty-seven years later, Mrs. Wilkes' Boarding House involves four generations of the family. They have traveled to New York, Brussels, and Tokyo promoting Southern food and hospitality for the state of Georgia.

Savannah is proud to be home to such a popular and long-lived establishment. Mrs. Wilkes and Grandmother Paul are definitely my two true heroes.

Mrs. Wilkes and her family send warm regards, and hope that you enjoy the following recipes from the cookbook *Famous Recipes from Mrs. Wilkes' Boarding House.*

Mrs. Wilkes' Boarding House–Style Biscuits

YIELDS ABOUT 16 BISCUITS

2 cups self-rising flour	2 tablespoons margarine
½ teaspoon baking powder	⅓ cup buttermilk
1 tablespoon vegetable shortening	⅓ cup milk

Preheat the oven to 450 degrees. Sift the flour and baking powder into a mixing bowl and make a well in the center. Cut in the shortening and margarine until the mixture resembles coarse cornmeal. Pour the buttermilk and milk into a measuring cup and add enough water to make ¾ cup. Pour this into the dry ingredients. Mix lightly and quickly with your hands to form a dough moist enough to leave the sides of the bowl. Turn the dough onto a lightly floured surface. Knead by turning the dough away from you, pressing down with palms of hands, and pushing the dough away. Repeat 6 or 7 times. Work the dough into a large ball while kneading; keep your fingers dry by dipping them into dry flour frequently. Pinch off portions of dough and place them on a well-greased baking sheet. Press lightly to flatten the biscuits slightly. Bake for 12 to 15 minutes, or until golden brown on top.

Baked Bean Casserole

SERVES 8

2 tablespoons bacon fat or
   vegetable oil
1 cup sliced onions
Two 1-pound cans Boston-style
   baked beans

1 cup diced cooked ham
1 tablespoon prepared mustard
2 tomatoes, peeled and sliced
2 teaspoons brown sugar
1 teaspoon salt

Preheat the oven to 400 degrees. Heat the fat in a heavy skillet, add the onions, and sauté until tender. Combine the beans, ham, and mustard; arrange half this mixture in a 2-quart casserole. Place half of the onions and tomatoes over the beans; sprinkle with half of the sugar and salt. Repeat with the remaining ingredients. Bake, covered, for 30 minutes. Uncover the casserole and bake for 5 minutes longer.

Beef Stew Casserole

SERVES 6

2 pounds beef stew meat
1 teaspoon salt
Pinch of pepper
⅓ cup all-purpose flour
2 tablespoons vegetable shortening
1 large onion, quartered
1 cup apple juice

2 medium unpeeled cooking
   apples, sliced
3 carrots, cut into long, narrow
   strips
1 cup diced celery
1 bay leaf
¼ teaspoon dried oregano

Sprinkle the meat with salt and pepper, then dredge it in the flour. Heat the shortening in a heavy skillet. Add the meat and cook until browned on all sides. Add the onion. Pour in the apple juice and bring to a boil. Cover and simmer for about 1½ hours, or until the meat is tender. Place the apples, carrots, and celery in a casserole, then pour the stew into the casserole. Add the bay leaf and oregano and bake at 350 degrees for 30 minutes. Remove and discard the bay leaf. Serve the stew over mashed potatoes or rice.

Elizabeth on 37th

Elizabeth on 37th opened in Savannah in May 1981, as the creation of chef Elizabeth Terry and her husband, Michael. The simple elegance of their turn-of-the-century Southern mansion sets the perfect tone for her stunning regional cooking.

Chef Terry is devoted to classic Southern cooking, and she has extensively researched Savannah cooking of the eighteenth and nineteenth centuries. She has combined traditional cooking methods with a modern interest in fresh, health-conscious menus.

Elizabeth Terry's reputation as an innovator and leader in the cuisine of the "New South" is well established. Her awards have been many.

We hope that you enjoy the recipes from Elizabeth's cookbook *Savannah Seasons: Food and Stories from Elizabeth on 37th.*

Fried Grits Cakes with Sausage

SERVES 6

1 pound hot bulk sausage
2 tablespoons grated orange zest
4 cups chicken broth

1 cup stone-ground yellow grits
Vegetable oil

In a large skillet over medium heat, combine the sausage and orange zest, stirring to break up the sausage. Sauté until browned and then drain; set aside.

In a large saucepan over medium heat, bring the chicken broth to a boil. Slowly stir in the grits. Reduce the heat, cover, and simmer for 20 minutes, stirring occasionally. Stir the sausage into the grits. Spread the mixture in a 13 × 9-inch baking pan to cool, then refrigerate until well chilled. Cut the chilled grits into squares and sauté in vegetable oil until crisp and browned on both sides.

Shrimp Bel Vedere

SERVES 6

2 cups new potatoes, cut into
 ½-inch dice
1 cup water
½ cup (1 stick) butter
2 pounds medium shrimp, peeled
 and deveined, tossed with
 1 tablespoon cornstarch
1¼ cups fresh corn kernels
 (from 3 ears)
3 green or poblano peppers, seeded
 and slivered

1 cup julienned Vidalia or other
 sweet onion
2 cups diced fresh tomatoes
18 whole small okra
2 bay leaves
¼ teaspoon cayenne pepper
½ teaspoon paprika
½ teaspoon salt

Put the potatoes and water in a large stockpot and bring to a boil over
high heat. Lower the heat to medium and cook for 15 minutes, or
until the potatoes are soft and the water almost gone. Stir in the butter and cook for 3 minutes longer, then stir in the shrimp, vegetables,
bay leaves, cayenne, paprika, and salt, increase the heat to high, and
cook, stirring occasionally, until the shrimp are just pink, about 5 minutes. Discard the bay leaves and serve immediately.

Blueberry Raspberry Pecan Crisp

SERVES 4

⅔ cup all-purpose flour
2 tablespoons rolled oats
⅓ cup packed brown sugar
½ teaspoon cinnamon
¼ cup (½ stick) cold butter, cubed
½ cup pecans, toasted

1 cup fresh raspberries or
 blackberries
½ cup granulated sugar
1 tablespoon cornstarch
4 cups fresh blueberries
2 tablespoons honey

Preheat the oven to 375 degrees.

For the topping, in the bowl of a food processor, combine the flour, oats, brown sugar, and cinnamon, and process briefly to mince the oats. Add the butter and process until the mixture looks moist and begins to stick together. Stir in the pecans. Transfer to a small bowl and refrigerate.

In a large saucepan over high heat, stir together the raspberries, granulated sugar, and cornstarch. Bring to a boil and cook, stirring, until the mixture is slightly thick and shiny, about 3 minutes. Stir in the blueberries and pour into a baking dish. Crumble the topping over the berries and bake for 30 minutes, or until golden. Remove the dish from the oven, drizzle the honey over the topping, and return to the oven for 5 minutes. Cool for at least 15 minutes before serving. Serve warm.

The Johnny Harris Restaurant

The Johnny Harris Restaurant is truly a Savannah institution. Located at 1651 East Victory Drive, it began life in 1936. Some say it had the first air-conditioned dining room in the South. Phil Donaldson, the owner, has worked in the restaurant in various capacities since the age of seven. Over the years Phil has had the privilege of meeting and feeding hundreds of thousands of people from all walks of life. When Jackie Gleason's train rumbled through Savannah it would stop long enough to send out for Johnny Harris's succulent spareribs.

Renowned songwriter Johnny Mercer, a Savannah native, always ate fried chicken in the restaurant's kitchen when he was in town. It's said that many nights, just before closing, he would place orders for fried chicken for his late evening card games. The list goes on and on, from Robert Mitchum to Bob Hope to John Berendt, who wrote in *Midnight in the Garden of Good and Evil* that while incarcerated Jim Williams would get supper from Johnny Harris's one night and Elizabeth on 37th the next.

I think, however, that what might please the gentlemanly Phil Donaldson the most is the multiple generations of hometown folks who continue to carry on the tradition of enjoying wonderful meals from Johnny Harris's.

Thanks ever so much for sharing with us, Phil—your food, your hospitality, and your recipes.

Steak au Poivre

SERVES 4

⅓ cup black peppercorns
Four ¾- to 1-inch thick strip steaks
5 tablespoons olive oil

2 tablespoons, plus 1 teaspoon butter
¼ cup minced shallots
¼ cup Cognac or brandy

½ cup rich beef broth
4 tablespoons chopped fresh
  tarragon

Salt and pepper

Crack the peppercorns by crushing them against a cutting board with the side of a heavy knife or the bottom of a pan. Press the peppercorns into both sides of the steaks. Heat the oil and 2 tablespoons of the butter in a heavy skillet. Cook the steaks to the desired doneness. Remove them from the pan and keep warm while you prepare the sauce. Add the shallots to the hot skillet and sauté until translucent. For the next step, be very careful as the Cognac will create a large flame. Add the Cognac or brandy to the pan. Light a match and touch flame to liquid. Stepping back, shake the pan above the burner until the flame dies out; add the broth and cook over very high heat. Whisk in the remaining teaspoon of butter and the tarragon. Season with salt and pepper to taste. Serve the sauce over the steaks.

Baked Flounder

SERVES 3–4

1½ pounds flounder fillets*
Salt and pepper
3 ounces sherry

1½ cups (2 sticks) melted butter
2 cups breadcrumbs

Preheat the oven to 375 degrees. Lay the flounder fillets in a buttered 13 × 9 × 2-inch baking dish. Season with salt and pepper to taste.

Pour the sherry over the fish, then pour on half of the butter. Cover the fish with breadcrumbs and pour the remaining butter over the crumbs. Bake for 15 minutes.

*Cooked lobster meat or raw scallops may be substituted for flounder.

Pasta Puttanesca Sauce

SERVES 4–6

Phil Donaldson writes: "This Italian sauce is probably the best-tasting spaghetti sauce we have ever tasted. However, it is not very well known. The name means 'prostitute's sauce,' and the story goes that the ladies would prepare the sauce and put it on their windowsills, and the smell was so fabulous that it attracted clients for them."

¼ cup olive oil
4 cloves garlic, crushed
Two 14½-ounce cans Italian plum tomatoes, coarsely chopped, juice reserved
½ cup sliced black olives
¼ cup dry red wine

¼ cup drained capers
8 anchovy fillets, minced
¼ cup chopped fresh Italian parsley or basil
1½ teaspoons dried oregano
½ teaspoon dried rosemary
⅛ teaspoon red pepper flakes

Heat the olive oil in a heavy skillet over medium heat. Sauté the garlic until translucent. Add the tomatoes and their reserved juice, then stir in the olives, wine, capers, anchovies, parsley, dried herbs, and pepper flakes.

Bring to a boil, cover, and reduce to a slow simmer. Simmer for 45 minutes. Serve over pasta.

Lucile Wright

This chapter would not be complete without a sampling of recipes from Mrs. Lucile Wright. Mrs. Wright just celebrated her ninety-first birthday and is no longer active in the food-service business, but to native Savannahians she remains a sweet memory of bygone days.

Miss Lucile was the most sought-after caterer in Savannah. Her food was in such high demand that parties were sometimes rescheduled to suit her availability. Firmly established as a local legend, Miss Lucile was made even more famous by the book *Midnight in the Garden of Good and Evil*. Page 8 in "The Book" will acquaint you with Mrs. Wright even more. Jim Williams loved to entertain and entertain he did, always quite lavishly. His Christmas party was the highlight of Savannah's social season, and the party would not be complete if the tables were not groaning with delectable bites provided by Miss Lucile. I wish to thank the Savannah *News Press* for supplying me with two of her famous recipes from the "Inside Close-ups" column.

Lucile Wright's Tomato Sandwiches

Bread: Use thin slices, whole wheat on the bottom, white on the top. Cut the bread into circles with a biscuit cutter, and remove the circle of bread. Prepare the bread a day ahead, if you like.

Spread: Mix a little grated onion (too much makes it bitter), black pepper, and Accent into Hellman's mayonnaise. No measurements here. Make it to taste. Spread the bread a day ahead. Cover and refrigerate.

Tomatoes: Peel, slice, and drain thoroughly between layers of paper towels. (Soggy tomatoes make soggy sandwiches.) Sprinkle the tomatoes with Lawry's Seasoned Salt before assembling the sandwiches. You may prepare the sandwiches several hours before a party. Cover with a damp tea towel and refrigerate.

Lucile Wright's Oyster Bisque

YIELDS 2½ QUARTS

1 quart oysters (extra pint
   optional)
Salt and black pepper
4 stalks celery, cut in medium-size
   pieces
1 medium onion, chopped
4 cups milk
2 cups heavy cream
4 tablespoons butter

4 tablespoons all-purpose flour
Freshly grated nutmeg
Curry powder
Accent
1 tablespoon fresh lemon juice
1 tablespoon Worcestershire sauce
Cayenne pepper
Paprika
Chopped fresh parsley

Pick over the oysters for shells. Simmer the oysters in a covered pot over low heat with a little salt and black pepper. Stir occasionally until the edges of the oysters curl. Lift the oysters out of the stock with a slotted spoon and put them in a colander with a bowl underneath to catch the pot liquor. Pour the stock from the pot into the bowl, being careful to discard any oyster dregs. Set the stock aside.

Cook the celery and onion in a little water until tender; drain, reserving the broth. Add the broth to the oyster stock (should measure about 2 cups), then add the milk and cream (reserve a little cream to whip for garnish).

Heat the butter, then whisk in the flour to make a roux. Add the stock mixture to the roux, and stir briskly until thickened and smooth. Add a little nutmeg, a pinch of curry powder, a pinch of Accent, the lemon juice, Worcestershire, and cayenne. Correct the seasonings. Mash the oysters with the celery and onions and mix well; add to oyster stock. Keep warm over hot water until time to serve. Whip the reserved cream. Pour bisque into individual bowls. Swirl an even portion of whipped cream into each bowl. Add a little paprika and chopped parsley to garnish. Offer sherry separately, if desired.

John Berendt

All of the people and places included in the Peers chapter of this book live in Savannah, with the exception of one. This person could not be more a part of this city if he had lived here a hundred years—and do tell, dearie, he's a Yankee! The man I'm talking about is noted author John Berendt, who brought fame to himself and Savannah with his highly acclaimed *Midnight in the Garden of Good and Evil*. If you haven't read "The Book," as we refer to it here in Savannah, by all means treat yourself to the talent of John's storytelling ability. I promise, you won't be disappointed.

John wrote the wonderful Introduction to my first book, *The Lady & Sons Savannah Country Cookbook*, for which I will always be grateful. It seems only fitting that I take this opportunity to formally thank you, John, for the support you gave me. Thank you from the bottom of my heart!

I felt this project wouldn't be complete without some of John's favorite recipes, so naturally I turned to his mother, Carol Berendt, who I knew was filled with love and pride for the son she affectionately calls Johnny. So, here we go, three of Johnny's and his mother's favorite recipes.

Fresh Cabbage and Sweet Sausages

SERVES 2

4 Italian-style sweet sausages, or
    4 unseasoned fresh pork sausages
2 potatoes, peeled and quartered
4 cups finely sliced green cabbage
½ cup water

Put sausages in a skillet, place potatoes between them, cover with cabbage, and add water. Cover and cook over very low heat, and forget about it until suppertime. It won't burn, but it will brown by itself. Serve with mustard and vinegar.

Lemon Hollandaise Sauce

YIELDS ½ CUP

John and his mother serve this wonderful sauce over roasted chicken breasts to make a delicious lemon chicken.

2 egg yolks
4 tablespoons cream
2 large tablespoons butter
Juice of ½ lemon

Pinch of salt
Pinch of sugar
Chicken broth (optional)

Combine all ingredients in the top of a double boiler, over boiling water. Stir until thick, approximately 3 minutes; set aside until ready to use. Do not reheat or cover the pot. Mrs. Berendt suggests thinning this out with a little chicken broth, if needed.

Pots de Crème

6 ounces semisweet chocolate chips
2 eggs
1 tablespoon sugar

1 tablespoon brandy
Pinch of salt
¾ cup milk

Put all ingredients except the milk in a blender. In a saucepan, over medium heat, heat the milk until very hot but not boiling. Add the milk to the blender and blend 20 seconds. Pour the mixture into 6 ramekins or demitasse cups and chill for at least 4 hours. Serve with whipped cream, if desired, or try using it as the filling in a pie, using a prebaked crust.

Desserts

CAKES AND PIES

Pear-Licious Cake

Chocolate Torte

Green Tomato Cake

Fourth-Generation Blackberry Jam Cake

Double-Dutch Chocolate Fudge Upside-Down Cake

Milky Way Cake

Sour Cream Caramel Cake

Texas Sheet Cake

Cheesecake with Praline Sauce

Caramel-Nut Pound Cake

Hummingbird Cake

Coconut Cream Cake

Mississippi Mud Cake

Orange Blossoms

Chocolate Chip Pound Cake

Red Velvet Pound Cake

Orange Slice Cake

Volcano Cake

Caramel Apple Cheesecake

Italian Love Cake

Coconut White Fruit Cake

Grandgirl's Fresh Apple Cake from Georgia

Pig Pickin' Cake

Turtle Cheesecake

Pecan Pudding Cake

Blueberry Cream Pie

Peanut Butter Pie

Lisa's Southern Pecan Pie

Cherry Cream Cheese Pie

Chocolate Cream Pie

Apple Crisp

Ritz Cracker Pie

Lemon Meringue Pie

Old-Fashioned Sweet Potato Pie

Key Lime Pie

Shaver's Chocolate Pecan Pie

Half-Million-Dollar Pie

Fried Apple Pies

Our Pear Cobbler

Old-Fashioned Fudge Pie

PUDDINGS AND CUSTARDS

Pumpkin Gingerbread Trifle

Old-Fashioned Rice Pudding

Crème Brûlée

Strawberry Cream Shortcake

Chocolate Trifle

English Trifle

Mexican Flan

Compote Clouds

Butterscotch Delight

Heavenly Banana Delight

Chocolate Bread Pudding

COOKIES AND BROWNIES

Sugar Cookies

Oatmeal Cookies

Hidden Kisses

Brown Sugar Cookies

Swedish Countess Cookies

Magical Peanut Butter Cookies

Brenda's Kahlúa Brownies

Pecan Pie Squares

Lemon Bars

Glazed Honey Bars

Chocolate Mound Brownies

Pear-Licious Cake

SERVES 16–20

CAKE

1¼ cups vegetable oil
2 cups granulated sugar
3 eggs
3 cups all-purpose flour
1 teaspoon salt
1 teaspoon baking soda
1 teaspoon cinnamon
1 teaspoon vanilla extract
2 cups chopped canned Bartlett
 pears in syrup, well drained
 (reserve syrup for glaze)
1 cup chopped pecans

GLAZE

1 tablespoon butter, at room
 temperature
1½ cups confectioners' sugar
2–3 tablespoons syrup from canned
 pears

Preheat the oven to 325 degrees. In a mixing bowl, combine the oil, sugar, and eggs, and beat well. Sift together the flour, salt, baking soda, and cinnamon. Add this to the creamed mixture and stir until blended. Stir in the vanilla. Fold in the pears and pecans. Grease and flour a 10-inch tube pan or Bundt pan, and spoon in the batter. Bake for 1 hour and 20 minutes, or until the cake tests done. Let the cake cool for 20 minutes, then turn it out onto a cake rack to cool completely. While the cake cools, make the glaze. Blend the butter and confectioners' sugar with enough of the reserved pear syrup to make a smooth, slightly runny glaze. Drizzle the glaze over the cake top, letting some run down the sides. ❦ ❦ ❦ **The Lady & Sons**

Chocolate Torte

SERVES 8

One 6-ounce package chocolate
   chips
¼ cup (½ stick) butter
¼ cup hot water
4 egg yolks
8 tablespoons cold water

8 tablespoons Kahlúa, sweet sherry,
   or amaretto
2 packages ladyfingers
1½ cups heavy cream
⅓ cup sugar

Combine the chocolate, butter, and hot water in the top of a double boiler. Place the pan over medium-high heat and cook until the chocolate and butter are melted. Add the egg yolks one at a time, stirring well after each; continue to stir for 2 minutes. Remove the pan from the heat. Combine the cold water and liqueur in a small bowl, and quickly dip the ladyfingers in this mixture. Line the bottom of a 9 × 5 × 3-inch loaf pan with ladyfingers, and pour half of the chocolate cream over them.

Add another layer of ladyfingers, the remaining chocolate cream, and another layer of ladyfingers. Refrigerate for at least 2 hours. Just before serving, whip the cream with the sugar until stiff. Unmold the torte onto a platter and frost it with the whipped cream.

Green Tomato Cake

SERVES 15–20

2¼ cups sugar
1 cup melted vegetable shortening
3 eggs
2 teaspoons vanilla extract
3 cups all-purpose flour
1 teaspoon salt
1 teaspoon baking soda

1 teaspoon cinnamon
½ teaspoon freshly grated nutmeg
1 cup chopped walnuts
1 cup raisins
2½ cups diced green tomatoes
1 small can Angel Flake coconut

Preheat the oven to 350 degrees. In a mixing bowl, cream the sugar, shortening, eggs, and vanilla until smooth.

Add the flour, salt, soda, and spices, and stir to blend. Stir in the nuts, raisins, and tomatoes. Grease a 9 × 13-inch pan. Pour the batter into the pan and sprinkle the coconut on top. Bake for 1 hour.

❧ ❧ ❧   *The Lady & Sons*

Fourth-Generation Blackberry Jam Cake

SERVES 15–18

CAKE
1 cup vegetable shortening
1⅓ cups granulated sugar
4 eggs
4 cups all-purpose flour
1 teaspoon baking powder
1 teaspoon baking soda
1 teaspoon salt
1 teaspoon ground allspice
1 teaspoon cinnamon
1 teaspoon freshly grated nutmeg

1 cup buttermilk
1 cup chopped pecans
1 cup raisins
2 cups blackberry jam

CARAMEL ICING
½ cup (1 stick) butter
1 cup packed brown sugar
¼ cup milk
2 cups confectioners' sugar, sifted

Preheat the oven to 350 degrees. Grease and flour two 10-inch round cake pans.

For the cake, in a mixing bowl, cream the shortening and granulated sugar until fluffy. Add the eggs one at a time, mixing well after each. Sift the flour with the baking powder, baking soda, salt, and spices. Add the flour mixture alternately with the buttermilk, beginning and ending with the flour. Stir in the nuts and raisins, then stir in the jam.

Pour the batter into the prepared pans and bake for 30 to 40 minutes, or until the cake pulls away from the pan. Cool the cakes in the pans for 10 minutes, the turn them out onto cake racks to cool completely.

While the cake cools, make the icing. Melt the butter in a saucepan, add the brown sugar, and bring to a boil. Boil over low heat for 2 minutes, stirring constantly. Add the milk and continue stirring until the mixture returns to a boil. Remove the pan from the heat and scrape the mixture into a mixing bowl. Let cool. Add the confectioners' sugar a little at a time, beating well after each addition, until the icing is thick enough to spread. Fill and ice the cake.

VARIATION: You may prefer to bake this cake in a tube pan: Pour the batter into the greased and floured pan and bake for 15 minutes, then reduce the heat to 300 degrees and bake for about 1 hour 15 minutes, or until the cake tests done. Cool as directed for the 10-inch layers.

Double-Dutch Chocolate Fudge Upside-Down Cake

SERVES 8–10

1 cup all-purpose flour
1 cup granulated sugar
2 tablespoons, plus ¼ cup cocoa
   powder
2 teaspoons baking powder
¼ teaspoon salt
½ cup milk

2 tablespoons vegetable oil or
   melted butter
1½ teaspoons vanilla extract
½ cup chopped walnuts (optional)
1 cup packed brown sugar
1½ cups boiling water
1 cup heavy cream

Preheat the oven to 350 degrees.

In a mixing bowl, stir together the flour, ¾ cup of the granulated sugar, 2 tablespoons of the cocoa powder, the baking powder, and the salt. Add the milk, the oil, and 1 teaspoon of the vanilla, and stir until blended. Stir in the nuts, if using. Pour the batter into a greased 9 × 13-inch pan.

In a small bowl, combine the brown sugar with the ¼ cup cocoa powder; stir well. Spread this mixture over the batter in the pan. Using a large spoon, drizzle the boiling water over the cake; do not stir. Bake for 40 to 45 minutes, or until the top of the cake is firm. Let the cake cool slightly. Meanwhile, whip the cream with the remaining ¼ cup granulated sugar and ½ teaspoon vanilla. Cut the cake into squares and place them upside down (gooey side up) on dessert plates. Spoon a dollop of whipped cream onto each piece of cake.

Milky Way Cake

SERVES 16–20

CAKE
Confectioners' sugar, for dusting
  pans
Eight 1¾-ounce Milky Way bars
1½ cups (3 sticks) butter
2 cups granulated sugar
4 eggs, well beaten
2½ cups all-purpose flour
¼ teaspoon baking soda
1¼ cups buttermilk
1 cup chopped pecans
1 teaspoon vanilla extract

ICING
2½ cups granulated sugar
1 cup evaporated milk
1 cup marshmallow cream
½ cup (1 stick) butter
6-ounces chocolate chips
1 cup chopped pecans

Preheat the oven to 325 degrees. Grease three 9-inch cake pans and dust them with confectioners' sugar. To make the cake, melt the Milky Way bars with 1 stick of butter. Remove from the heat and let cool. Cream the remaining 2 sticks of butter with the granulated sugar. Add the beaten eggs and the cooled chocolate mixture. Sift the flour and the baking soda together. Alternately add the flour and buttermilk to the batter, blending well. Add the nuts and vanilla. Divide the batter among the prepared pans and bake for 30 to 40 minutes, or until the cake is firm to the touch. Cool for 5 minutes, remove from the pans, and place on cooling racks. While the cake cools, prepare the icing: Combine the sugar and milk in a heavy saucepan. Cook to the soft-ball stage (234 degrees on a candy thermometer). Remove the pan from the heat and add the marshmallow cream, butter, and chocolate chips, stirring until melted. Add the pecans. When the cake has cooled completely, frost each layer, sides, and the top of the Milky Way Cake.

❦ ❦ ❦ **The Lady & Sons**

Sour Cream Caramel Cake

SERVES 15–20

CAKE
1 cup (2 sticks) butter
3 cups granulated sugar
6 eggs
2⅔ cups all-purpose flour
1 teaspoon salt
¼ teaspoon baking soda
1 cup sour cream
1 tablespoon vanilla extract

EASY CARAMEL ICING
2 cups packed dark brown sugar
1 cup (2 sticks) butter
½ cup evaporated milk
½ teaspoon vanilla extract
4 cups confectioners' sugar

Preheat the oven to 350 degrees. Grease and flour three 9-inch round cake pans or one 13 × 9-inch pan. For the cake, cream the butter and granulated sugar until fluffy. Add the eggs one at a time, beating after each addition. Sift the flour, salt, and baking soda together. Alternately add the flour mixture and the sour cream to the batter, stirring well. Stir in the vanilla. Pour the batter into the prepared pans and bake for 25 to 35 minutes or until firm to the touch if using round pans, 45 minutes if using the rectangular pan. Let the cakes cool in the pans for a few minutes, then turn them out onto cake racks to cool completely.

While the cakes cool, make the icing: In a large, heavy saucepan, combine the brown sugar, butter, and milk. Cook over low heat until the butter melts. Increase the heat to medium and cook, stirring constantly, for 2 minutes longer. Remove the pan from the heat and stir in the vanilla. Gradually mix in the confectioners' sugar. Let the icing cool slightly, then frost the cooled cake.   ❧ ❧ ❧   *The Lady & Sons*

Texas Sheet Cake

SERVES 20–24

CAKE
1 cup (2 sticks) butter
1 cup water
4 tablespoons cocoa powder
2 cups all-purpose flour
2 cups granulated sugar
1 teaspoon baking soda
½ teaspoon salt
2 eggs
½ cup sour cream

ICING
½ cup (1 stick) butter
6 tablespoons milk
4 tablespoons cocoa powder
1 pound confectioners' sugar,
   sifted
1 teaspoon vanilla extract
1 cup chopped pecans (optional)

Preheat the oven to 350 degrees. For the cake, combine the butter, water, and cocoa in a saucepan, and bring to a boil. Remove from the heat. In a mixing bowl, mix together the flour, granulated sugar, baking soda, and salt. Add the butter mixture all at once, and stir to blend. Whisk the eggs and sour cream together; add to the batter and mix well. Pour the batter into an 18 × 12 × 1-inch pan and bake for 20 minutes.

Just before the cake is done, make the icing: Combine the butter, milk, and cocoa in a large, heavy saucepan and bring to a boil. Add the confectioners' sugar and vanilla, and mix well. Ice the cake while it is still warm, and top with nuts if desired. ❦ ❦ ❦ *The Lady & Sons*

Cheesecake with Praline Sauce

SERVES 12

CRUST

1½ cups graham cracker crumbs
4 tablespoons granulated sugar
¼ cup (½ stick) melted butter

FILLING

Three 8-ounce packages cream
   cheese, at room temperature
1 cup granulated sugar
5 eggs
1 tablespoon vanilla extract

TOPPING

1½ cups sour cream
4 tablespoons granulated sugar
1 teaspoon vanilla extract

PRALINE SAUCE

2 tablespoons light brown sugar
2 tablespoons cornstarch
1 cup dark corn syrup
½ cup chopped pecans
1 teaspoon vanilla extract

Preheat the oven to 350 degrees.

For the crust, stir together the graham cracker crumbs, sugar, and butter. Pat this mixture into the bottom and sides of a 9-inch spring-form pan.

Make the filling: In a large bowl, beat together the cream cheese and granulated sugar. Beat in the eggs, one a time, then beat in the vanilla. Pour the filling into the crust and bake for 1 hour. Remove the cake from the oven and cool for 10 minutes.

Meanwhile, make the topping: In a bowl, mix the sour cream, sugar, and vanilla until well blended. Spread this mixture over the warm cake and return to the oven for 5 minutes. Let the cake cool to room temperature in the pan, then cover with plastic wrap and refrigerate for at least 4 hours, or overnight.

At serving time, use a table knife to loosen the cake from the pan. Remove the sides of the pan and place the cake on a platter, leaving it on pan bottom. To make the praline sauce, in a small heavy saucepan stir together the brown sugar and cornstarch. Stir in the corn syrup and cook over medium heat, stirring constantly, until thick. Remove the pan from the heat and stir in the nuts and vanilla. Cool slightly.

Serve the cheesecake, passing the sauce in a bowl with a small ladle. Store any leftovers in the refrigerator.   ❈ ❈ ❈ *The Lady & Sons*

Caramel-Nut Pound Cake

SERVES 16–20

1 cup (2 sticks) butter
½ cup vegetable shortening
1 pound light brown sugar
1 cup granulated sugar
5 large eggs
3 cups all-purpose flour

½ teaspoon baking powder
½ teaspoon salt
1 cup milk
1 cup chopped pecans
1 tablespoon vanilla extract

Preheat the oven to 325 degrees. In a mixing bowl, cream the butter and shortening. Beat in the brown sugar a little at a time. Add the granulated sugar and beat until light and fluffy. Add the eggs one at a time, beating well after each addition. Sift the flour with the baking powder and salt. Alternately add the flour mixture and the milk to the batter, blending well. Stir in the nuts and vanilla.

Bake in a greased and floured tube pan for 1½ hours. Cool for 10 to 15 minutes and invert onto serving platter. 🌸 🌸 🌸 **The Lady & Sons**

Hummingbird Cake

SERVES 18–20

CAKE
3 cups all-purpose flour
2 cups granulated sugar
1 teaspoon baking soda
1 teaspoon cinnamon
½ teaspoon salt
3 eggs, beaten
¾ cup vegetable oil
1¾ cups mashed bananas
One 8-ounce can crushed
    pineapple, with juice
1 cup chopped pecans
1½ teaspoons vanilla extract

FROSTING
One 8-ounce package cream cheese,
    at room temperature
½ cup (1 stick) butter, at room
    temperature
1 pound confectioners' sugar,
    sifted
1 teaspoon vanilla extract
½ cup chopped pecans

Preheat the oven to 350 degrees. Grease and flour three 9-inch round cake pans. For the cake, in a mixing bowl, stir together the flour, sugar, baking soda, cinnamon, and salt. Add the eggs and oil and stir just until the dry ingredients are moistened. Do *not* beat. Stir in the banana, the pineapple and its juice, the pecans, and the vanilla. Divide the batter among the prepared pans and bake for 23 to 28 minutes, or until a wooden pick inserted in the center comes out clean. Cool the cake layers in the pans for 10 minutes, then turn them out onto a rack to cool completely.

While the cake cools, make the frosting: In a bowl, blend together the cream cheese and butter. Gradually add the confectioners' sugar, beating until light and fluffy. Beat in the vanilla. Stir in the pecans, or reserve them to sprinkle over the frosted cake. Fill and frost the cake.

❦ ❦ ❦   *The Lady & Sons*

Coconut Cream Cake

SERVES 20

This cake is worth the wait. The longer it sits the better it tastes.

CAKE

1 cup (2 sticks) butter, at room
   temperature
2 cups granulated sugar
5 eggs
3½ cups all-purpose flour
3 teaspoons baking powder
1 cup milk
2 teaspoons vanilla extract

FILLING

1 cup chilled heavy cream
2 cups sour cream
2 cups confectioners' sugar
1 teaspoon vanilla extract
3 cups shredded coconut, plus more
   for topping
One 12-ounce container Cool
   Whip (optional)

Preheat the oven to 350 degrees. Grease and flour three 9-inch round pans. For the cake, cream the butter and granulated sugar until light and fluffy. Add the eggs one at a time, beating well after each addition. Combine the flour and baking powder; add to the creamed mixture alternately with the milk, beginning and ending with flour. Stir in the vanilla. Divide the batter among the prepared pans and bake for 25 to

30 minutes, or until firm to the touch. Cool the cakes for 10 minutes in the pans, then turn them out to cool completely.

While the cakes cool, make the filling: In a large chilled bowl, whip the heavy cream until stiff. Fold in the sour cream, then gradually add the confectioners' sugar. Stir in the vanilla, then fold in the coconut.

To serve, split each cake layer in half horizontally. Spread the filling between the layers and on top of the cake. Place the cake in an airtight container and refrigerate for 3 days before serving. When ready to serve, remove from refrigerator and sprinkle with coconut. If desired, frost with Cool Whip. ❧ ❧ ❧ **The Lady & Sons**

Mississippi Mud Cake

SERVES 15–20

CAKE

2 cups granulated sugar
1 cup vegetable shortening
4 eggs
1½ cups all-purpose flour
⅓ cup cocoa powder
1¼ teaspoons salt
1 cup chopped walnuts
3 teaspoons vanilla extract
One 10½-ounce package
   miniature marshmallows

ICING

¾ cup (1½ sticks) butter, at room
   temperature
1 pound confectioners' sugar
⅓ cup cocoa powder
½ cup evaporated milk
1 cup chopped walnuts
1 teaspoon vanilla extract

Preheat the oven to 300 degrees. For the cake, in a mixing bowl, cream the granulated sugar and shortening well. Add the eggs and beat well. Sift the flour, cocoa powder, and salt together. Stir the flour mixture into the creamed mixture. Add the nuts and vanilla. Pour the batter into a greased 9 × 13-inch pan and bake for 30 minutes. Remove from the oven and cover the top of the cake with the marshmallows. Return the cake to the oven and bake for about 10 minutes longer, or until the marshmallows melt. While the cake is baking, make the icing: Beat the butter, confectioners' sugar, and cocoa, until creamy. Slowly beat in the milk. Stir in the nuts and vanilla. Ice the cake while it is still warm.

❧ ❧ ❧ **The Lady & Sons**

Orange Blossoms

YIELDS 7–8 DOZEN

CAKES
1 package yellow cake mix
One 3.4-ounce package instant
 lemon pudding mix
4 eggs
¾ cup cold water
¾ cup vegetable oil

GLAZE
3 cups confectioners' sugar
½ cup frozen orange juice
 concentrate, thawed
3 tablespoons melted butter
3 tablespoons water

Preheat the oven to 325 degrees. Grease one or two miniature muffin pans. For the cakes, in a mixing bowl, combine the cake mix, pudding mix, eggs, water, and oil, and beat well. Fill the prepared muffin pans, using about 1 tablespoon of batter for each cake. Bake for 10 to 12 minutes, or until the cakes spring back when touched.

For the glaze, mix the confectioners' sugar, orange juice, butter, and water until smooth; set aside.

Dip the blossoms in the glaze immediately after removing them from the oven. Drain on waxed paper.

Chocolate Chip Pound Cake

SERVES 16

4 eggs
1½ cups water
1 teaspoon vanilla extract
1 package butter recipe cake mix
One 3.4-ounce package instant
 vanilla pudding mix

One 3.4-ounce package instant
 chocolate pudding mix
½ cup (1 stick) melted butter
¼ cup vegetable oil
6-ounces chocolate chips
Confectioners' sugar, for dusting

Preheat the oven to 350 degrees. Grease and flour a tube pan or bundt pan. In a mixing bowl, beat the eggs, water, and vanilla by hand. Stir in the cake mix and pudding mixes. Slowly add the butter and oil, and mix well. Stir in the chocolate chips. Pour into the prepared pan.

Bake for 50 to 60 minutes. Cool for 10 minutes, then invert onto a cake plate. Sift confectioners' sugar over the cake, or drizzle chocolate sauce over it, if desired. ❦ ❦ ❦ *The Lady & Sons*

Red Velvet Pound Cake

SERVES 16

CAKE

1 cup (2 sticks) butter, at room
  temperature
½ cup vegetable shortening
3 cups granulated sugar
7 eggs
One 1-ounce bottle red food
  coloring
2 teaspoons vanilla extract
3 cups cake flour
¼ teaspoon salt
1 cup milk

FROSTING

Two 3-ounce packages cream
  cheese, at room temperature
½ cup (1 stick) butter, at room
  temperature
1 teaspoon vanilla extract
One 1-pound package
  confectioners' sugar, sifted
1–2 tablespoons milk, if needed

Preheat the oven to 325 degrees. Grease and flour a 10-inch tube pan. For the cake, in a mixing bowl, combine the butter, shortening, and sugar, and cream until light and fluffy. Add the eggs one at a time, beating well after each addition. Stir in the food coloring and vanilla. Stir together the flour and salt; add this to the creamed mixture alternately with the milk, beating well. Pour the batter into the prepared pan. Bake 1 hour and 20 minutes, or until a toothpick inserted in the center comes out clean. Cool the cake in the pan for 10 minutes, then turn it out onto a rack to cool completely.

While the cake cools, make the frosting: Combine the cream cheese and butter and blend until smooth. Stir in the vanilla, mixing well. Gradually add the sugar, beating until creamy. If necessary, add a little milk to achieve a spreading consistency.

Frost the cake.

Orange Slice Cake

SERVES 15–20

CAKE
4 cups all-purpose flour
½ teaspoon baking soda
1 pound candy orange slices
One 8-ounce package pitted dates
2 cups chopped pecans
1 cup shredded coconut
1 cup (2 sticks) butter
2 cups granulated sugar

4 eggs
1 teaspoon baking soda
½ cup buttermilk

GLAZE
1 cup confectioners' sugar
2 tablespoons orange juice
1 teaspoon grated orange zest

Preheat the oven to 300 degrees. Grease a 10-inch tube pan. For the cake, sift together 3½ cups of the flour and the baking soda. Cut the orange slices and dates into small pieces and add them with the remaining ½ cup flour. Add the nuts and coconut; set aside. Cream the butter and sugar. Add the eggs and beat well. Stir the baking soda into the buttermilk. Alternately add the flour and the buttermilk mixture, beginning and ending with flour. Fold in the candy mixture. Pour the batter into the prepared pan and bake for 1¾ to 2 hours, or until a wooden pick inserted in the center comes out clean. Cool the cake in the pan for 10 minutes, then turn the cake out of the pan onto a rack.

To make the glaze, stir together the confectioners' sugar, orange juice, and zest.

Drizzle the glaze over the warm cake.　❦ ❦ ❦　*The Lady & Sons*

Volcano Cake

SERVES 12–16

1 cup shredded coconut
1 cup chopped walnuts or pecans

1 package German chocolate cake mix

10 bite-size Almond Joy candy
    bars, chopped
One 8-ounce package cream cheese,
    at room temperature

½ cup (1 stick butter), at room
    temperature
2 cups confectioners' sugar

Preheat the oven to 350 degrees. Spray a 13 × 9 × 2-inch pan with nonstick cooking spray. Mix the coconut and nuts and spread them evenly in the pan. Prepare the cake mix as directed on the box. Stir in the chopped candy bars. Pour the batter over the coconut and nuts. Combine the cream cheese, butter, and sugar. Randomly drop tablespoonfuls of this on top of the batter; do not spread them. Bake for 40 to 50 minutes, or until sides of the cake pull away from the pan.

This cake is wonderful served warm or cool with a dollop of whipped cream.   🍃 🍃 🍃 **The Lady & Sons**

Caramel Apple Cheesecake

SERVES 8

One 21-ounce can apple pie filling
One 9-inch graham cracker crust
Two 8-ounce packages cream
    cheese, at room temperature
½ cup sugar

¼ teaspoon vanilla extract
2 eggs
¼ cup caramel topping
12 pecan halves, plus 2 tablespoons
    chopped pecans

Preheat the oven to 350 degrees. Reserve ¾ cup of the apple filling; set aside. Spoon the remaining filling into the crust. Beat together the cream cheese, sugar, and vanilla until smooth. Add the eggs and mix well. Pour this over the pie filling. Bake for 35 minutes, or until the center of the cake is set. Cool to room temperature. Mix the reserved pie filling and caramel topping in a small saucepan and heat for about 1 minute, or until spreadable. Spoon the apple-caramel mixture over the top of the cheesecake and spread evenly. Decorate the edge of the cake with pecan halves and sprinkle with chopped pecans. Refrigerate the cake until ready to serve.

Italian Love Cake

SERVES 15–20

CAKE
2 pounds ricotta cheese
4 eggs
¾ cup sugar
1 teaspoon vanilla extract
1 package fudge marble cake mix

ICING
One 5.1-ounce package instant
   chocolate pudding mix
1 cup cold milk
8 ounces Cool Whip

Preheat the oven to 350 degrees. Grease and flour a 13 × 9-inch pan. For the cake, mix the ricotta, eggs, sugar, and vanilla; set aside. Prepare the cake mix according to package directions and pour it into the prepared pan. Immediately spread the ricotta mixture directly on top of the batter. Bake for 1 hour. Remove from the oven and let cool completely in the pan.

For the icing, stir the pudding mix into the milk, then fold in the Cool Whip. Spread the icing on the cake in the pan and refrigerate overnight. ❦ ❦ ❦ **The Lady & Sons**

Coconut White Fruit Cake

SERVES 16–20

7 egg whites
1 cup candied cherries
1 cup candied pineapple
1 pound golden raisins
4 cups pecans, chopped
2 cups all-purpose flour
½ teaspoon salt

1 cup (2 sticks) butter, at room
   temperature
2 cups sugar
One 6-ounce package frozen
   grated coconut
1 teaspoon vanilla extract

Preheat the oven to 325 degrees. Line the bottom of a tube or loaf pan with brown paper and grease the paper. In a large bowl, beat the egg whites until stiff peaks form, and set aside. In another large bowl, combine the candied fruits, raisins, and nuts. Add the flour and salt, and toss to mix; set aside. Cream the butter and sugar. Add the beaten egg whites, then the coconut and vanilla. Add the fruit to the coconut mixture. Pour the batter into the prepared pan and bake for 2¼ hours.

Grandgirl's Fresh Apple Cake from Georgia

SERVES 16–20

CAKE
2 cups sugar
3 eggs
1½ cups vegetable oil
¼ cup orange juice
3 cups all-purpose flour
1 teaspoon baking soda
¼ teaspoon salt
1 tablespoon cinnamon
1 tablespoon vanilla extract

3 cups peeled and finely chopped
   apples
1 cup shredded coconut
1 cup chopped pecans

SAUCE
½ cup (1 stick) butter
1 cup sugar
½ cup buttermilk
½ teaspoon baking soda

Preheat the oven to 325 degrees. Generously grease a tube pan. For the cake, combine all the cake ingredients in a large bowl in the order given and mix well. Pour the batter into the prepared pan and bake for 1½ hours.

Shortly before the cake is done, make the sauce: Melt the butter in a large saucepan, stir in the sugar, buttermilk, and baking soda, and bring to a good rolling boil, stirring constantly. Boil for 1 minute. Pour the sauce over the hot cake in the pan as soon as you remove it from the oven. Let stand 1 hour, then turn out.

Pig Pickin' Cake

SERVES 16–20

CAKE

1 box yellow cake mix
One 11-ounce can mandarin
   oranges, with juice
4 eggs
¼ cup vegetable oil

FROSTING

One 16-ounce can crushed
   pineapple, drained
One 3.4-ounce package instant
   vanilla pudding mix
Two 8-ounce containers Cool
   Whip, or 1 quart heavy cream,
   whipped and sweetened with 1
   cup sugar

Preheat the oven to 350 degrees. Grease and flour three 8-inch round pans. Mix together the cake mix, the oranges with their juice, eggs, and oil. Divide the batter among the prepared pans; layers will be thin. Bake for 15 to 20 minutes, or until the cake tests done. Cool the layers on wire racks.

While the cake cools, make the frosting: Mix the drained pineapple with the pudding mix and fold this mixture into the Cool Whip. Fill and frost the cooled cake layers. Refrigerate until ready to serve.

❦ ❦ ❦   *The Lady & Sons*

Turtle Cheesecake

SERVES 12

CRUST

3 cups chocolate wafer crumbs
¼ cup sugar
⅓ cup melted butter

FILLING

Three 8-ounce packages cream
   cheese, at room temperature
1¼ cups sugar
4 large eggs

1 cup sour cream
1 tablespoon vanilla extract

TOPPING

¼ cup (½ stick) butter
6 ounces chocolate chips
One 12-ounce jar caramel topping
   (Smucker's makes a good one)
1 cup chopped pecans

Preheat the oven to 325 degrees. Lightly grease a 9-inch springform pan. In a bowl, combine the wafer crumbs, sugar, and butter; stir well. Firmly press the mixture on the bottom and 1 inch up the sides of the prepared pan. Bake for 10 minutes. Cool on a wire rack.

For the filling, beat the cream cheese with an electric mixer on medium speed until creamy. Gradually add the sugar, beating well. Add the eggs one at a time, beating well after each addition and scraping the sides and bottom of the bowl as needed. Stir in the sour cream and vanilla. Pour the batter into the prepared crust. Bake for 1 hour and 5 minutes. (Center of cake will not be completely set.) Turn the oven off and partially open the oven door. Leave the cheesecake in the oven for 1 hour. Remove to a wire rack to cool completely. Cover the cake and refrigerate for at least 8 hours. Carefully remove the sides of the pan and transfer the cake to a platter.

For the topping, melt the butter in a small heavy saucepan. Add the chocolate chips and stir over low heat just until the chocolate melts and blends with the butter. Spread the warm chocolate mixture over the cheesecake; refrigerate for 15 minutes.

Combine the caramel topping and pecans in a small saucepan. Bring to a boil, over medium heat, stirring constantly, and boil for 2 minutes. Remove from the heat and cool for 5 minutes, then spread over the chocolate and cool completely. Serve right away, or cover and chill. Refrigerate any leftovers. 🌸 🌸 🌸 *The Lady & Sons*

Pecan Pudding Cake

SERVES 15–20

CAKE
1 package yellow cake mix
1 cup milk
4 eggs
⅓ cup vegetable oil
1 cup chopped pecans

TOPPING
2 cups cold milk
One 3.4-ounce package instant
   vanilla pudding mix

One 8-ounce package cream cheese,
   at room temperature
2 cups heavy cream
6 tablespoons sugar
One 26-ounce can crushed
   pineapple, with juice
½ cup chopped pecans
½ cup coconut flakes

Preheat the oven to 350 degrees. Grease and flour a 13 × 9 × 2-inch pan. In a bowl, combine the cake mix, milk, eggs, oil, and pecans, and blend just until moistened; then beat at medium speed for two minutes. Pour the batter into the prepared pan and bake for 30 to 35 minutes, or until a wooden pick comes out clean.

While the cake is baking, make the topping: Stir together the milk and the pudding, then beat in the cream cheese, a few small pieces at a time; set aside. Whip the cream with the sugar until stiff.

When the cake is done, prick the top with a fork. Pour the pineapple and juice over the hot cake. Spread the cream cheese mixture over the pineapple, then cover the cake with the whipped cream. Garnish the cake with the pecans and coconut. Refrigerate for a while. The longer the cake is refrigerated the better it tastes. This cake freezes well.

Blueberry Cream Pie

SERVES 6–8

¾ *cup chopped pecans or walnuts*
One *9-inch deep-dish pie crust*
 (*thawed if frozen*)
Two *3-ounce packages cream*
 cheese, at room temperature

1 cup confectioners' sugar
1 cup heavy cream
¼ *cup granulated sugar*
One *21-ounce can blueberry pie*
 filling

Press the chopped nuts into the bottom of the pie crust. Bake as directed on the package and let cool. Beat the cream cheese with the confectioners' sugar. Beat the heavy cream with the granulated sugar until it forms soft peaks. Fold the whipped cream into the cream cheese mixture. Spoon this mixture into the cooled pie shell and top with blueberry pie filling. Refrigerate until well chilled. ❧ ❧ ❧ **The Lady & Sons**

Peanut Butter Pie

SERVES 6

One 3-ounce package cream cheese
1 cup confectioners' sugar
½ cup peanut butter
¼ cup evaporated milk

1½ cups Cool Whip
One 8-inch graham cracker crust
⅓ cup chopped peanuts

Whip the cream cheese until fluffy, then beat in the sugar and peanut butter. Slowly add the milk, blending well. Fold the Cool Whip into the cream cheese mixture and spoon this into the pie crust. Sprinkle with peanuts. 🐾 🐾 🐾 **The Lady & Sons**

Lisa's Southern Pecan Pie

SERVES 6–8

Lisa, our head chef and night kitchen manager, whips these pies up fresh daily for our guests in the restaurant. They go great with our homemade vanilla ice cream.

4 tablespoons butter
¾ cup packed brown sugar
1 tablespoon all-purpose flour
¼ teaspoon salt
¾ cup cane syrup

3 eggs
1 teaspoon vanilla extract
1 cup pecan halves
One 9-inch pie crust

Preheat the oven to 325 degrees. Cream the butter, sugar, flour, and salt until smooth. Add the syrup, eggs, and vanilla, then fold in the pecans. Pour the filling into the pie crust and bake for 45 to 50 minutes or until firm to the touch.

Serve the pie warm or cool. 🐾 🐾 🐾 **The Lady & Sons**

Cherry Cream Cheese Pie

SERVES 6–8

One 8-ounce package cream cheese,
at room temperature
One 14-ounce can sweetened
condensed milk
½ cup fresh lemon juice

1 teaspoon vanilla extract
One 9-inch graham cracker crust
One 21-ounce can cherry pie
filling, chilled

In a mixing bowl, beat the cream cheese until light and fluffy. Gradually add the milk; stir until well blended. Stir in the lemon juice and vanilla. Pour the filling into the crust and refrigerate for 2 to 3 hours. Top with the pie filling before serving.   ❧ ❧ ❧   **The Lady & Sons**

Chocolate Cream Pie

SERVES 6–8

FILLING
1 cup sugar
3 tablespoons cocoa powder
2 tablespoons all-purpose flour
Pinch of salt
3 egg yolks, beaten
2 cups milk
1 tablespoon butter

1 teaspoon vanilla extract
One 9-inch baked pie crust

MERINGUE
3 egg whites
¼ teaspoon cream of tartar
4 tablespoons sugar

For the filling, in a saucepan, stir together the sugar, cocoa, flour, and salt. Slowly stir in the beaten yolks and the milk. Cook over low heat, stirring constantly, until the mixture thickens. Remove from the heat and stir in the butter and vanilla. Pour the filling into a bowl to cool. Pat waxed paper onto the surface of the filling to prevent a crust from forming. When cool, pour the filling into the pie crust.

Preheat the oven to 350 degrees. Make the meringue: Beat the egg whites with the cream of tartar until they form soft peaks. Add 1 tablespoon of sugar at a time, beating constantly, until the whites form stiff peaks. Spoon the meringue over the pie filling, spreading it out to touch the crust all around. Bake until brown, 10 to 12 minutes.

Apple Crisp

SERVES 8

6 large apples (about 2½ pounds),
   peeled, cored, and thinly sliced
¼ cup water
Juice of 1 lemon
2 cups rolled oats

2 cups all-purpose flour
2 cups packed brown sugar
2 tablespoons cinnamon
1¼ cups (2½ sticks) melted butter

Preheat the oven to 350 degrees. Combine the apples, water, and lemon juice in an 8 × 8-inch baking pan. In a bowl, combine the oats, flour, sugar, and cinnamon. Pour in the butter and stir to make a crumbly mixture. Spread the topping in an even layer over the apples and bake for 45 to 55 minutes, or until the topping is crisp and browned.

Ritz Cracker Pie

SERVES 6–8

This is an old family recipe. It really is a pie—as it bakes, it makes its own crust.

3 egg whites
1 teaspoon baking powder
1½ cups sugar
20 Ritz Crackers, crumbled

1½ cups chopped pecans
1 teaspoon vanilla extract
2 cups heavy cream

Preheat the oven to 325 degrees. Grease a 9-inch pie pan. Beat the egg whites with the baking powder until stiff. Blend in 1 cup of the sugar, then add the cracker crumbs, pecans, and vanilla. Pour into the prepared pie pan and bake for 30 minutes. Meanwhile, whip the cream with the remaining ½ cup sugar until thick and spreadable. When the pie is done, place it on a rack to cool completely. Spread the whipped cream over the cooled pie.

Lemon Meringue Pie

SERVES 6

1½ cups sugar
Pinch of salt
3 tablespoons cornstarch
1½ cups cold water
4 egg yolks, lightly beaten
Grated zest of 1 lemon

½ cup fresh lemon juice
1 tablespoon butter
One 9-inch prebaked pie crust
4 egg whites
½ teaspoon cream of tartar

Preheat the oven to 350 degrees. For the filling, in a 2-quart saucepan, stir together 1 cup of the sugar, the salt, and cornstarch. Gradually stir in the water until smooth. Add the egg yolks, stirring constantly. Bring to a boil over medium heat and boil for 1 minute. Remove from the heat. Stir in the lemon zest, lemon juice, and butter, and set aside to cool. Turn the filling into the pie crust.

For the meringue, in a small bowl, with an electric mixer on high speed, beat the egg whites and cream of tartar until foamy. Add the remaining ½ cup of sugar 1 tablespoon at a time, beating well after each addition. Continue beating until stiff peaks form.

Spread some meringue around the edge of the filling first, touching the crust all around. Then fill the center with meringue. Bake for 15 to 20 minutes or until the meringue is lightly browned. Cool the pie at room temperature away from drafts.

Old-Fashioned Sweet Potato Pie

SERVES 6–8

2 cups peeled, cooked, mashed sweet
   potatoes*

1¼ cups sugar
¼ cup (½ stick) melted butter

*Mash the sweet potatoes with an electric mixer. This will produce a smooth, creamy pie with no lumps.

2 eggs
1 teaspoon vanilla extract, or
   1–2 tablespoons bourbon
¼ teaspoon salt
¼ teaspoon cinnamon

¼ teaspoon ground ginger
1 cup milk
One 9-inch unbaked pie crust
3 egg whites

Preheat the oven to 350 degrees. For the filling, in a large bowl, combine the potatoes, 1 cup of the sugar, the butter, eggs, vanilla, salt, and spices. Mix thoroughly. Add the milk, stirring well. Pour the mixture into the pie crust and bake for 40 to 50 minutes, or until a knife inserted in the center comes out clean. Place the pie on a rack and cool to room temperature before covering with meringue.

For the meringue, using an electric mixer, beat the egg whites until soft peaks form; beat in the remaining ¼ cup sugar 1 tablespoon at a time. Continue beating until the sugar dissolves and the mixture is glossy and stiff, but not dry. With a rubber spatula, spoon the meringue onto the pie, forming peaks. Make sure the meringue touches the crust all around. Sprinkle with a pinch of granulated sugar. Bake for 5 to 10 minutes, or until delicately browned. Cool and serve.

Key Lime Pie

SERVES 6

A true Key lime pie should not be green!

One 14-ounce can sweetened
   condensed milk
½ cup Key lime juice
1 teaspoon grated lime zest
3 eggs, separated

One 8-inch prebaked pie crust or
   graham cracker crust
¼ teaspoon cream of tartar
¼ cup sugar

Preheat the oven to 325 degrees. In a medium bowl, combine the milk, lime juice, and zest; blend in the egg yolks. Pour the filling into the crust. For the meringue, beat the egg whites with the cream of tartar until soft peaks form. Gradually beat in the sugar until the mixture is stiff. Spread the meringue over the filling; spread it to touch the edge of the crust all around. Bake for 12 to 15 minutes, or until the meringue is golden brown.

Shaver's Chocolate Pecan Pie

SERVES 6–8

½ cup (1 stick) butter
2 squares (2 ounces) semisweet
  chocolate
2 eggs, well beaten
½ cup sugar
½ cup light corn syrup

¼ cup all-purpose flour
1 teaspoon vanilla extract
⅛ teaspoon salt
¾ cup chopped or whole pecans
  (depending on your preference)
One 9-inch unbaked pie crust

Preheat the oven to 325 degrees. Melt the butter and chocolate in a double boiler over hot water. Pour this into a bowl and add the beaten eggs, then stir in the sugar, corn syrup, flour, vanilla, and salt. Fold in the pecans. Pour the filling into the crust and bake for about 30 minutes. Watch carefully and do not take the pie out of the oven until the top looks dry. You can make up to 4 pies at one time. They freeze beautifully. Serve with whipped cream or vanilla ice cream on top, if you like.

Half-Million-Dollar Pie

SERVES 16–20

One 14-ounce can sweetened
  condensed milk
¼ cup fresh lemon juice
One 11-ounce can mandarin
  oranges, drained and chopped

One 8-ounce can crushed
  pineapple, drained
1 cup chopped pecans
One 16-ounce carton Cool Whip
2 graham cracker pie crusts

In a bowl, mix the milk and lemon juice. Stir in the oranges, pineapple, and pecans. Fold the Cool Whip into the fruit mixture. Divide the filling between the pie crusts. Cover and refrigerate. Refrigerated, the pies will keep for up to 8 days.

Fried Apple Pies

YIELDS 8 PIES

*My grandmother Irene Paul taught me to make fried pies years ago. She made the pastry dough from scratch in the early days, but later in life she began to take advantage of modern conveniences. So here's the recipe for Grandmother's updated but old-fashioned fried pies.**

One 5-ounce package dried apples (or any other dried fruit)
2 cups water
½ cup sugar
2 tablespoons butter
½ teaspoon cinnamon

One 15-ounce package refrigerated pie crust (found in dairy section)
1½ cups vegetable oil, or more as needed

Cook the apples with the water in a covered pot over medium-low heat for about 1 hour, or until all liquid has been absorbed. Stir occasionally. Add the sugar, butter, and cinnamon, mixing well; set aside to cool. Unfold the pie crust and break into 8 equal pieces like pie slices. Place 1 heaping tablespoon of fruit on each round of dough, leaving a ½-inch border all around. Dip your finger in water and moisten the edges of the crust, then place a second round on top of the filling and press the edges to seal. Dip the tines of a dinner fork in flour and crimp the edges to ensure a proper seal.

Pour the oil into a cast-iron skillet to a depth of a little less than ½ inch. (This would be 1½ cups oil in a 10-inch skillet.) Heat over medium-high heat. When the oil is hot, place 3 to 4 pies in the skillet and cook for about 2 minutes on each side, or until golden brown. Drain on paper towels. Repeat until all the pies are cooked, or wrap and freeze some of the uncooked pies for another day.

Sprinkle the pies with granulated sugar while they're hot.

*For super-quick fried pies, use canned apple pie filling and canned biscuits that have been rolled out into a 5- or 6-inch round. Shape and cook pies as directed.

Our Pear Cobbler

SERVES 8

This cobbler is sooo good and sooo easy. It's unbeatable topped with vanilla ice cream. You can substitute peaches or pineapple tidbits for the pears.

½ cup (1 stick) butter
1 cup sugar
¾ cup self-rising flour

¾ cup milk
One 29-ounce can pear halves in
　heavy syrup

Place the butter in a baking dish and place in a 350-degree oven until the butter has melted. Leave the oven on. Stir together the sugar and flour; slowly stir in the milk and mix well. Pour the batter over the melted butter in the pan. *Do not stir.* Break the pears in half and place them on top of the batter; gently pour the syrup from the pears over the cobbler. *Do not stir.* Bake the cobbler for 30 minutes.

❦ ❦ ❦　**The Lady & Sons**

Old-Fashioned Fudge Pie

SERVES 6–8

2 squares (2 ounces) semisweet
　chocolate
½ cup (1 stick) butter

1 cup sugar
2 eggs, beaten
One 9-inch unbaked pie crust

Preheat the oven to 375 degrees. Melt the chocolate and butter together in a heavy saucepan over low heat. Remove the pan from the heat and add the sugar, then the eggs; beat well. Pour the filling into the pie crust and bake for 25 minutes. Serve warm or cold, with ice cream or whipped cream.

Pumpkin Gingerbread Trifle

SERVES 20

Two 14-ounce packages
  gingerbread mix
One 5.1-ounce package cook-and-
  serve vanilla pudding mix
One 30-ounce can pumpkin pie
  filling

½ cup packed brown sugar
⅓ teaspoon ground cardamom or
  cinnamon
One 12-ounce carton Cool Whip
½ cup gingersnaps (optional)

Bake the gingerbread according to the package directions; cool completely. Meanwhile, prepare the pudding and set aside to cool. Stir the pumpkin pie filling, sugar, and cardamom into the pudding.

Crumble one batch of gingerbread into the bottom of a large, pretty bowl. Pour ½ the pudding mixture over the gingerbread, then add a layer of Cool Whip. Repeat with the remaining gingerbread, pudding, and Cool Whip. Sprinkle the top with crushed gingersnaps if desired. Refrigerate overnight. Can be layered in a punch bowl.

❦ ❦ ❦   **The Lady & Sons**

Old-Fashioned Rice Pudding

SERVES 8–10

My friend Damon Fowler, chef and author, taught me the importance of using freshly grated nutmeg. The difference is remarkable, so please don't substitute ground nutmeg from a jar. Grate the nutmeg on the fine side of your grater, being careful that you don't include a little knuckle! Fresh nutmeg can be found right next to the ground nutmeg in your local supermarket.

1 cup sugar

2 tablespoons all-purpose flour

½ teaspoon salt

2 cups milk

3 egg yolks

2⅓ cups cooked white rice

⅓ cup raisins

¼ cup (½ stick) butter

2 teaspoons vanilla extract

2 teaspoons fresh lemon juice

¼ teaspoon freshly grated nutmeg

3 egg whites, at room temperature

¼ teaspoon cream of tartar

4 tablespoons sugar

Preheat the oven to 350 degrees. In a saucepan, mix the sugar, flour, and salt. Slowly stir in the milk. Cook over medium-low heat, stirring constantly, until thickened. Beat the egg yolks lightly, then stir in about ½ cup of the hot custard to temper the eggs. Add the egg mixture to the custard and cook for 2 minutes longer, stirring constantly.

Remove from the heat and stir in the rice, raisins, butter, vanilla, lemon juice, and nutmeg. Pour into a greased 1½-quart casserole and bake for 20 to 25 minutes. Five minutes before the pudding is done, make the meringue: Beat the egg whites and cream of tartar in a deep, narrow bowl until the egg whites form soft peaks. Add 1 tablespoon of sugar at a time, beating well after each addition.

Remove the pudding from the oven and top with the meringue, swirling it into peaks. Bake for 12 to 15 minutes longer, or until browned. ❦ ❦ ❦ *The Lady & Sons*

Crème Brûlée

SERVES 4

2 cups heavy cream

1 vanilla bean, split lengthwise

4 large egg yolks

¼ cup, plus 1 tablespoon granulated sugar

⅓–½ cup white granulated or light brown sugar

Preheat the oven to 300 degrees. In a heavy-bottomed medium nonreactive saucepan, heat the cream with the vanilla bean for 15 minutes, stirring to ensure it does not burn. Remove from the heat and let steep for 15 minutes. Remove and discard the vanilla bean. Strain the cream. Meanwhile, in a medium bowl, beat the egg yolks with an electric mixer on high speed for 5 minutes, or until they are light and fluffy. Gradually beat in the granulated sugar. Add about half the cream mixture, a little at a time, to the egg mixture, whisking until well blended. Then pour the egg mixture into the remaining cream mixture. Stir until completely blended.

Pour the custard into four 8-ounce ramekins or custard cups. Place the dishes in large baking pan. Pour enough hot water into the pan to come halfway up the sides of the ramekins. Bake for 35 to 40 minutes or until the mixture is set in the center (it should still wiggle when shaken). Remove the dishes from the baking pan. Let cool completely at room temperature, then refrigerate for at least 2 or up to 24 hours.

Let the ramekins stand at room temperature 20 minutes before serving. Spoon the ⅓ to ½ cup white or light brown sugar in a thin, even layer over each portion of custard, covering it completely. To caramelize the sugar, light a propane torch and hold it so the flame just touches the surface. Start at the center and spiral out toward the edges of the ramekins. If the sugar begins to burn, pull the torch away and blow on the sugar to extinguish the flame.

VARIATIONS: Finely grate orange zest or bittersweet chocolate over the crème before adding the sugar for caramelizing. A propane torch can be bought at your local hardware store. If you don't have one, caramelize the topping under the broiler, watching carefully so as not to burn it.

Strawberry Cream Shortcake

SERVES 8–10

1 large Sara Lee Pound Cake
One 5.1-ounce package vanilla
   instant pudding mix
1½ cups water
1 cup sweetened condensed milk

1 teaspoon vanilla extract
One 12-ounce container Cool
   Whip
2 cups strawberries, hulled and
   sliced

Slice the cake very thin and lay half the slices in a 13 × 9-inch glass baking dish. In a bowl, combine the pudding mix, water, milk, and vanilla with an electric mixer. Fold in the Cool Whip. Pour half of this over the cake and lay half of the strawberries on top. Repeat to make a second layer.

Refrigerate until well chilled.

Chocolate Trifle

SERVES 20–25

This recipe evolved quite by accident in the restaurant kitchen on a particularly harried day. The baker had put a pan of blond brownies in the oven, and in the rush had left them in too long. When I looked at them, and then at her, our faces fell—the brownies were burned. But we had to have that dessert. "Don't worry," I told her, "I'll think of something." I knew I had to act quickly to get the desserts to the table. So I cut the brownies into pieces and carefully trimmed off the burned edges. I crumbled up the good part, sprinkled it with sherry, covered it with chocolate pudding and topped it with fresh whipped cream—and our Chocolate Trifle was born. Today it is one of our most requested desserts. Hope y'all enjoy. Oh, by the way, you really don't have to go to the trouble of burning the brownies!

3 eggs
½ cup (1 stick) butter
1 pound light brown sugar
2 cups self-rising flour

1 tablespoon vanilla extract
2 cups chopped almonds
6 ounces chocolate chips

1 cup shredded coconut (optional)   *¼ cup sherry*
Two 3.4-ounce packages cook-and-   *2 cups heavy cream*
   serve chocolate pudding mix   *½ cup granulated sugar*

Preheat the oven to 375 degrees. Grease and flour a 13 × 9 × 2-inch pan. In a bowl, beat the eggs and butter together; add the brown sugar, then gradually add the flour and mix well. Stir in the vanilla. Fold in the nuts, chocolate chips, and coconut (if using). Spread the batter in the prepared pan and bake for 25 to 30 minutes. Cool and cut into squares.

Prepare the pudding according to the package directions. Let cool slightly. Crumble the brownies into chunks, put them back into the glass dish, and sprinkle with sherry. Spoon the pudding over the brownies. Beat the cream with the granulated sugar until stiff. Spoon the whipped cream onto the completely cooled trifle. Refrigerate until serving time.   ❦ ❦ ❦ **The Lady & Sons**

English Trifle

SERVES 12

CUSTARD
6 egg yolks
⅔ cup sugar
4 tablespoons cornstarch
2 cups milk
2 teaspoons vanilla extract

FRUIT MIXTURE
1 pineapple, peeled, cored, and cut
2 cups strawberries, hulled and
   sliced

2 bananas, peeled and sliced
2 kiwifruit, peeled and sliced
½ cup Triple Sec
6 ladyfingers
3 tablespoons raspberry jam

WHIPPED CREAM
1 cup heavy cream
1¼ cups sugar

First, make the custard: In a bowl, beat the egg yolks and sugar until light. Stir in the cornstarch. In a saucepan, scald the milk (do not boil it). Whisk the hot milk into the yolk mixture, then pour this back into the pan. Cook, stirring, over low heat until the custard thickens. Remove the pan from the heat and stir in the vanilla. Pour the custard into a bowl and set aside to cool completely.

While the custard cools, combine the cut-up fruit with the Triple Sec. Set aside to macerate for 30 minutes.

Spread the flat sides of the ladyfingers with jam, and place them in the bottom of a pretty glass bowl. Spoon the fruit and any liquid over the ladyfingers. Pour the cooled custard over the fruit. Refrigerate, covered, until the custard has set.

Beat the cream with the sugar until it holds a fairly stiff peak. Spread the whipped cream over the chilled custard, reserving some of the cream to pipe decoratively through a pastry tube, if desired.

Mexican Flan

SERVES 8

8 eggs
⅔ cup granulated sugar
¼ teaspoon salt
Two 12-ounce cans evaporated
    milk

1 teaspoon vanilla extract or
    brandy
½ cup packed brown sugar

Preheat the oven to 350 degrees. In a large bowl, beat the eggs well until fluffy. Beat in the sugar and salt, then beat in the milk. Stir in the vanilla. Sift the brown sugar into the bottom of a 5 × 9-inch loaf pan, covering the entire bottom. Carefully pour the custard into the pan. Place the loaf pan in a 13 × 9 × 2-inch pan and pour in enough hot water to reach halfway up the sides of the pan. Bake for 1 hour, or until a knife blade inserted in the center comes out clean. Let cool, then refrigerate overnight. Unmold the flan onto a platter.

Compote Clouds

SERVES 8

One 8-ounce package cream cheese,
    at room temperature
7 tablespoons sugar
One 8-ounce can crushed
    pineapple, drained, juice
    reserved

1 cup heavy cream
½ cup slivered almonds, toasted
½ cup fresh blueberries
¼ cup drained maraschino cherry
    halves

Beat the cream cheese with 3 tablespoons of the sugar until fluffy. Gradually add ¼ cup of the reserved pineapple juice and continue to beat until smooth. In another bowl, beat the cream with the remaining 4 tablespoons of sugar until it forms stiff peaks. Fold the whipped cream into the cream cheese mixture along with the pineapple, almonds, blueberries, and cherries. Refrigerate for 2 to 3 hours, or until well chilled. For a very pretty dessert, spoon the "clouds" into a stemmed glass compote.

Butterscotch Delight

SERVES ABOUT 15

2 cups graham cracker crumbs
½ cup (1 stick) melted butter
⅓ cup, plus ¾ cup granulated
    sugar
One 8-ounce package cream cheese,
    at room temperature
1 cup confectioners' sugar

3 cups heavy cream
Two 3.4-ounce packages
    butterscotch instant pudding
    mix
3 cups milk
Chopped peanuts (optional)

Preheat the oven to 350 degrees. For the crust, in a bowl, mix the graham cracker crumbs, butter, and ⅓ cup of the granulated sugar. Press this into the bottom of a 13 × 9 × 2-inch pan. Bake for 10 minutes; let cool. Beat the cream cheese with the confectioners' sugar. In another bowl, whip the cream with the remaining ¾ cup granulated sugar until it forms stiff peaks.

Prepare the pudding according to the package directions, using the 3 cups of milk.

Fold 1 cup of the whipped cream into the cream cheese mixture and spread this over the crust. Spread the pudding over the cream cheese layer.

Cover the pudding with the remaining whipped cream. Garnish with chopped peanuts, if desired.　　❧ ❧ ❧　***The Lady & Sons***

Heavenly Banana Delight

SERVES 10–12

One 3½-ounce package vanilla instant pudding mix	1 cup heavy cream
	1 cup sour cream
One 14-ounce can sweetened condensed milk	One 12-ounce box vanilla wafers
	3 or 4 bananas, sliced
1 cup milk	3 tablespoons chocolate syrup

In a large mixing bowl, combine the pudding mix, condensed milk, and milk, and beat for 2 minutes, or until well blended. Refrigerate for 10 minutes. In another bowl, whip the heavy cream. Add the whipped cream and sour cream to the pudding mixture. Place half the vanilla wafers in the bottom of a 13 × 9 × 2-inch dish. Top with half the sliced bananas, half the pudding mixture, and a drizzle of chocolate syrup. Repeat each layer and decorate the top with the remaining chocolate syrup.　　❧ ❧ ❧　***The Lady & Sons***

Chocolate Bread Pudding

SERVES 10–12

This simple, old-fashioned dessert is for chocolate lovers everywhere! Serve it warm or cold, with whipped cream or a dessert sauce.

One 1-pound loaf French or
    Italian bread, cut into cubes
    (about 15 cups)
3 cups milk
¼ cup heavy cream
½ cup coffee-flavored liqueur, such
    as Kahlúa
1 cup granulated sugar

1 cup packed light brown sugar
¼ cup Hershey cocoa powder
1 tablespoon vanilla extract
2 teaspoons pure almond extract
1½ teaspoons cinnamon
6 large eggs, lightly beaten
8 ounces semisweet chocolate,
    grated

Preheat the oven to 325 degrees. Lightly grease a 13 × 9-inch baking dish. Place the bread in the baking dish.

In a large bowl, whisk together the milk, cream, and liqueur. In another bowl, combine the granulated and brown sugars with the cocoa powder and mix well. Add this to the milk mixture and whisk to combine. Add the vanilla and almond extracts and the cinnamon to the beaten eggs. Combine the egg mixture with the milk mixture and mix well.

Stir in the grated chocolate. Pour the mixture evenly over the bread cubes; let stand, stirring occasionally, for at least 20 minutes, or until the bread has absorbed most of the milk mixture.

Bake the pudding for 1 hour, or until set; a knife inserted into the center of the pudding should come out clean.

Serve the pudding warm, or refrigerate it and serve chilled.

Sugar Cookies

YIELDS 5 DOZEN COOKIES

1½ cups confectioners' sugar, sifted
1 cup (2 sticks) butter
1 egg
1 teaspoon vanilla extract

1 teaspoon pure almond extract
2½ cups all-purpose flour
1 teaspoon baking soda
1 teaspoon cream of tartar

In a bowl, cream together the sugar and butter, then mix in the egg and the vanilla and almond extracts. In another bowl, stir together the flour, baking soda, and cream of tartar; mix the dry ingredients into the creamed mixture, then cover and refrigerate for 2 to 3 hours, or overnight.

Preheat the oven to 375 degrees. Divide the chilled dough in half and roll it out on a lightly floured pastry cloth to a ¼-inch thickness. Lightly grease some baking sheets. Cut the dough with a floured cookie cutter; sprinkle with sugar. Transfer the cookies to the prepared sheets and bake for 9 minutes.

Oatmeal Cookies

YIELDS ABOUT 45 LARGE COOKIES

*1 cup (2 sticks) butter, at room
    temperature*
1 cup granulated sugar
1 cup packed light brown sugar
2 eggs
1 teaspoon vanilla extract
2 cups all-purpose flour
1 teaspoon baking soda

½ teaspoon baking powder
¼ teaspoon salt
*½ teaspoon freshly grated nutmeg
    (optional)* *
2½ cups quick-cooking oats
1½ cups chopped walnuts
1 cup raisins

Preheat the oven to 375 degrees. Lightly grease some baking sheets. In a large bowl, cream the butter with the granulated and brown sugars until light and fluffy. Add the eggs, one at a time, beating well. Stir in the vanilla. In another bowl, mix the flour, baking soda, baking powder, salt, and nutmeg, if using. Beat the flour mixture into the creamed mixture. Stir in the oats, nuts, and raisins. Drop the dough by heaping tablespoons 2 inches apart on the prepared baking sheets. Bake for 10 to 12 minutes, or until golden brown.

*Do not substitute ground nutmeg for freshly grated. Omit if not available.

Hidden Kisses

YIELDS 3½–4½ DOZEN COOKIES

1 cup (2 sticks) butter, at room
    temperature
⅔ cup sugar
½ teaspoon vanilla extract
¼ teaspoon pure almond extract

1¾ cups all-purpose flour
¾ cup finely chopped pecans
One 9-ounce package Hershey's
    Kisses
1½ cups confectioners' sugar

In a large bowl, cream the butter, sugar, and vanilla and almond extracts. Stir in the flour and blend well. Add the pecans and blend well. Cover the bowl and refrigerate the dough for 1 hour. Preheat the oven to 375 degrees.

Unwrap the Hershey's Kisses. Press a scant tablespoon of dough around each Kiss, covering it completely; shape into balls.

Place the cookies on ungreased cookie sheets and bake for 10 minutes. Cool slightly, then transfer to a rack to cool completely. Roll the cookies in confectioners' sugar.

Brown Sugar Cookies

YIELDS ABOUT 4½ DOZEN COOKIES

1 cup (2 sticks) butter, at room
    temperature
2 cups packed brown sugar
2 tablespoons vanilla extract

2 eggs
2 cups self-rising flour
2 cups chopped walnuts or pecans

Preheat the oven to 375 degrees. In a bowl, cream the butter and sugar, then beat in the vanilla. Add the eggs one at a time, beating well. Add the flour ½ cup at a time, continuing to beat. Stir in the nuts.

Drop the dough by heaping tablespoon onto ungreased cookie sheets. Bake for 10 to 12 minutes, until golden brown.

VARIATION: For variety you may want to add chocolate chips or coconut flakes. Sometimes I add both, depending on my mood.

Swedish Countess Cookies

YIELDS 30–40 COOKIES

This recipe was found in a handwritten Swedish cookbook, dated about 1864, belonging to Countess Frida Af Trampe. This was said to be her favorite cookie. Ingrid Albertzon Parker, who is Swedish, took the time to translate this recipe into American measurements. I had the pleasure of having Ingrid come into my kitchen one afternoon to teach me the art of making these buttery little morsels. They are really very simple to make. The optional Cognac and shaved chocolate were added by Ingrid.

10 tablespoons (1¼ sticks) butter	1 tablespoon Cognac (optional)
¾ cup sugar	Shaved chocolate (optional)
1¼ cups all-purpose flour	

Preheat the oven to 350 degrees. Grease some baking sheets. Using an electric mixer, cream the butter until fluffy and white (about 5 minutes). Add the sugar and continue to beat. Add the flour a little at a time. Add the Cognac, if using, and mix well. Pinch off a piece of dough about the size of an egg. If the dough is sticky, sprinkle the work surface with a little flour. Place the piece of dough on the work surface. With your palms, roll the dough back and forth to form a rope of dough about as thick as your finger. Using your fingers, start at one end and flatten the dough to form a strip about 1¼ inches wide. Cut the dough on the diagonal into 2½-inch-long strips. They should be roughly diamond-shaped. Slip a knife blade under the dough and transfer to a greased baking sheet. Repeat until all the dough is used. Sprinkle a little shaved chocolate over each cookie, if desired. Bake for 8 to 10 minutes. These cookies should not brown, but should remain an off-white color.

Magical Peanut Butter Cookies

YIELDS 18 COOKIES

You won't believe how good this easy cookie is. For a change, press a Hershey's Kiss down into the center of each ball of dough. Omit the crisscross design.

1 cup peanut butter, creamy or crunchy
1⅓ cups sugar

1 egg
1 teaspoon vanilla extract

Preheat the oven to 350 degrees. Grease a large baking sheet. In a mixing bowl, combine the peanut butter, 1 cup of the sugar, the egg, and vanilla, and stir well with a spoon. Roll the dough into balls the size of walnuts. Place the balls on the prepared baking sheet. With a fork, press a crisscross design on each cookie. Bake for 12 minutes, remove from the oven, and sprinkle the cookies with some of the remaining sugar. Cool slightly before removing from pan.

Brenda's Kahlúa Brownies

YIELDS 2 DOZEN BROWNIES

⅔ cup butter
3 squares (3 ounces) unsweetened chocolate
1½ cups all-purpose flour, sifted
½ teaspoon baking powder

½ teaspoon salt
3 large eggs
2 cups sugar
½ cup, plus 1 tablespoon Kahlúa
¾ cup chopped walnuts or pecans

Preheat the oven to 350 degrees. Grease a 9 × 9-inch baking pan. Melt the butter and chocolate in the top of a double boiler over boiling water. Let cool slightly. Sift together the flour, baking powder, and salt; set aside. Beat the eggs with the sugar until light. Stir in the chocolate mixture and ½ cup of the Kahlúa, then add the flour mixture and blend. Stir in the nuts. Turn the batter into the prepared pan and bake for 30 minutes. When the brownies have cooled, brush the top with the remaining 1 tablespoon of Kahlúa.

Pecan Pie Squares

YIELDS 3 DOZEN BARS

1 box yellow cake mix
½ cup (1 stick) melted butter
4 eggs
1½ cups light corn syrup

½ cup packed dark brown sugar
1 teaspoon vanilla extract
2 cups chopped pecans

Preheat the oven to 350 degrees. Grease a 13 × 9-inch pan. For the crust, in a bowl mix the cake mix, butter, and 1 egg. Measure out ⅔ cup of this mixture and reserve it for the topping. Pat the remaining mixture into the bottom of the prepared pan and bake for 15 minutes.

Meanwhile, stir together the reserved crust mixture, the remaining 3 eggs, the corn syrup, sugar, and vanilla. Stir in the pecans. Pour this mixture over the partially baked crust. Increase the oven heat to 375 degrees and bake for 30 minutes, or until the cake is set. Let cool, then cut into bars.   ❧ ❧ ❧ **The Lady & Sons**

Lemon Bars

YIELDS 24 BARS

CRUST
2 cups all-purpose flour
1 cup confectioners' sugar
Pinch of salt
1 cup (2 sticks) butter, at room
   temperature

FILLING
4 eggs
2 cups granulated sugar
6 tablespoons all-purpose flour
6 tablespoons fresh lemon juice

Preheat the oven to 350 degrees. Lightly grease a 13 × 9 × 2-inch pan. Make the crust: Combine the flour, confectioners' sugar, and salt in a large bowl. Cut in the butter to make a crumbly mixture. Press the mixture into the prepared pan. You may need to dip your fingers into a little flour or confectioners' sugar to keep the dough from sticking to your fingers. Bake for 20 minutes. Meanwhile, make the filling: Mix the eggs, granulated sugar, flour, and lemon juice. Pour this over the baked crust and bake for 25 minutes longer. Sprinkle with confectioners' sugar, if desired, when the bars are done.   ✿ ✿ ✿   **The Lady & Sons**

Glazed Honey Bars

YIELDS ABOUT 2 DOZEN BARS

¾ *cup vegetable oil*
¼ *cup honey*
1 *cup granulated sugar*
1 *egg*
1 *teaspoon cinnamon*
2 *cups self-rising flour*

1 *cup chopped walnuts*
1 *cup confectioners' sugar*
1 *tablespoon mayonnaise*
1 *tablespoon milk*
1 *teaspoon vanilla extract*

Preheat the oven to 350 degrees. Lightly grease a $13 \times 9 \times 2$-inch pan. In a mixing bowl, beat the oil, honey, granulated sugar, and egg. Stir the cinnamon into the flour. Stir this into the sugar mixture and mix well. Stir in the nuts. Spread the batter in the prepared pan and bake for 30 minutes. Remove from the oven and let stand a few moments while you make the glaze: In a bowl, stir together the confectioners' sugar, mayonnaise, milk, and vanilla. Pour the glaze over the cake and spread it with a metal spatula. Let cool, then cut into bars.   ✿ ✿ ✿   **The Lady & Sons**

Chocolate Mound Brownies

SERVES 15–20

4 *squares (4 ounces) unsweetened*
   chocolate
1 *cup (2 sticks) butter*
4 *eggs, beaten*
2 *cups sugar*
2 *teaspoons vanilla extract*

1 *cup all-purpose flour*
1 *teaspoon baking powder*
¼ *teaspoon salt*
2 *cups chopped pecans*
1 *cup shredded coconut*

Preheat the oven to 350 degrees. Grease a 13 × 9-inch baking dish. In a large saucepan, or in the microwave, melt the chocolate and butter. Add the eggs, sugar, and vanilla, and stir well. Stir in the flour, baking powder, and salt, then add the pecans and coconut and stir until well blended. Pour the batter into the prepared baking dish and bake for 30 minutes. Cut into squares to serve.　　　❦ ❦ ❦　*The Lady & Sons*

Weights and Measures

All measurements given are level, unless otherwise specified.

1 cup—½ pint
2 cups—1 pint—1 pound
2 pints—1 quart—2 pounds
4 quarts—1 gallon—8 pounds
16 ounces—1 pound
1 fluid ounce—2 tablespoons
16 fluid ounces—1 pint
1 teaspoon—⅓ tablespoon
1 tablespoon—3 teaspoons
4 tablespoons—¼ cup
8 tablespoons—½ cup
1 cup—½ pint
8 quarts—1 peck
4 pecks—1 bushel
2 tablespoons butter—
    1 ounce
2 cups butter—1 pound
1 stick butter—½ cup

1 square baking chocolate—
    1 ounce
1 cup grated cheese—4 ounces
4 cups coarsely chopped nuts—
    1 pound
2⅓ cups uncooked rice—
    1 pound
1 cup uncooked rice—3½ cups
    cooked
2 cups granulated sugar—
    1 pound
2¼ cups packed brown sugar—
    1 pound
3½ cups sifted confectioners'
    sugar—1 pound
1 pound raw ground meat—
    2 cups
1 tablespoon liquid—½ ounce

Index